# THE CASE AGAINST CHRISTIAN NATIONALISM

Why "Taking America Back for God" Is Betraying Jesus, Breaking the Nation, and Fueling Project 2025

By

**L James Johnson**

Disclaimer:

This book is for educational and informational purposes only. Every effort has been made to ensure accuracy and completeness; however, no warranty is expressed or implied. The author and publisher are not engaged in rendering legal, financial, medical, or other professional advice. Readers should consult qualified professionals before acting on any information contained herein. The author and publisher disclaim any liability for loss or damage arising directly or indirectly from the use or application of any information in this book. The views expressed are solely those of the author and do not necessarily reflect the official policies or positions of any affiliated organization.

Unless otherwise noted, all Scripture quotations are taken from the World English Bible.

Cover and interior design by Tatjana W. (Upwork)

Published in the United States of America by Lone Wolf Consortium Publishing, LLC

Contact:

hello@TheJesusPrinciple.com

TheJesusPrinciple.com

TheJesusPrinciple.substack.com

ISBN: 978-1-935736-18-9

# TABLE OF CONTENTS

# DEDICATION

For all who refuse to bow to fear, who defend the vulnerable, tell the truth, and labor—often at great personal cost—for democracy, dignity, and the rule of law in this fragile moment of our republic.

# INTRODUCTION

In churches across America, millions of faithful Christians are sitting in pews, scrolling through social media, and listening to sermons that blend the language of Jesus with the language of political power. They hear calls to "take America back for God," to restore "biblical values" in law and culture, and to defend a "Christian nation" against enemies both foreign and domestic. For many, these messages feel like faithfulness, like standing up for what's right in a world that has lost its way.

But what if the very movement claiming to save America for God is actually leading us away from Jesus?

This book is written for every Christian who has felt that uneasy tug in their spirit when political rhetoric wraps itself in Scripture. It's for pastors navigating congregations split down the middle, for parents worried about their children's faith, and for anyone outside the church who wants to understand why Christian nationalism is not the same thing as Christianity. It's for people who love their country and want to engage faithfully in public life, but who sense that something has gone terribly wrong when the way of Jesus gets confused with the quest for political dominance.

The Jesus Principle is introduced as a simple, repeatable tool to help Christians discern whether they are moving toward or away from the character and teaching of Jesus. It takes four questions straight from Scripture—Does it bear good fruit? Does it care for the vulnerable? Does it follow the Golden Rule? Is it true?—and uses them as a filter for any claim made in Jesus' name. Rather than asking whether a position matches a party platform or talk radio narrative, the Jesus Principle asks whether it matches the life and words of Jesus himself, a framework explored more fully in my earlier book *The Jesus Principle: Are You Moving Toward Jesus—or Away?*, and applied specifically to Christian nationalism in the pages that follow.

Throughout this book, you'll meet Marcus, a composite character representing countless real Christians who have found themselves at a crossroads. Marcus is a sincere believer, a churchgoer, a man who loves his family and his country. He's also someone who has absorbed years of Christian nationalist messaging without realizing it was an ideology all along. As we walk through each chapter, you'll see Marcus gradually wake up to the conflict between the political project he's been sold and the Jesus he thought he was following. His journey is not a story of losing faith—it's a story of finding it again, freed from the distortions of nationalism, fear, and power.

This is not a book about Republicans versus Democrats. It's a book about Christian nationalism versus the way of Jesus. It's not a partisan rant; it's a pastoral invitation to test everything—including our own assumptions—against the life and teaching of the one we claim to follow. And it's grounded in history, evidence, and the lived experience of real people whose bodies, families, and freedoms are at stake when faith gets weaponized for political control.

If you've ever wondered whether "biblical values" politics actually reflects the Bible, whether "taking America back for God" is something Jesus would recognize, or how to talk with loved ones who have embraced Christian nationalism without losing the relationship, this book is for you. It will equip you to see more clearly, to speak more truthfully, and to live a public faith that looks less like a quest for dominance and more like the radical, self-giving love of Jesus.

Welcome to the journey. Let's begin where Marcus begins: in the pew, on an ordinary Sunday morning, when everything he thought he knew about faith and country is about to be tested.

# CHAPTER 1.

# MARCUS IN THE PEW: "TAKE AMERICA BACK FOR GOD"

Around Marcus, heads nodded. A few amens punctuated the silence. The words felt familiar, woven into so many sermons over the past few years that Marcus had stopped noticing when worship had become a rallying cry. This morning, though, something was different. Maybe it was the way Pastor Rick lingered over the phrase "biblical government," his voice dropping to a reverent hush as if he were speaking the name of God himself. Maybe it was the stack of policy briefs on the welcome table in the foyer, titled "A Christian Vision for America's Future," with bullet points that read less like theology and more like a political platform. Or maybe it was simply that Marcus had been reading the Gospels on his own lately—really reading them, not just skimming the red letters—and the Jesus he was meeting there didn't quite match the Jesus being invoked from the pulpit.

Pastor Rick was building to his main point now, describing a detailed agenda to "restore Christian values" to every level of government: new restrictions on abortion and contraception, rollbacks of protections for LGBTQ+ individuals, tighter immigration enforcement, expanded religious exemptions that would allow Christian business owners to refuse service, and a sweeping effort to rewrite school curricula to emphasize America's "Christian foundations." He called it God's blueprint for national renewal. He said it was what the Bible demanded.

He said faithful Christians had no choice but to support it, to vote for it, to fight for it.

Marcus felt the familiar swell of pride because his church was bold, unashamed, and willing to stand for truth in a culture that had lost its way. But underneath that pride, a quieter feeling stirred, one he could not quite name. It was not doubt, exactly. It was more like a question forming at the edges of his mind, a question he was not sure he wanted to ask out loud.

The sermon ended with a prayer for the nation and a call to action. As the congregation stood to sing the closing hymn, Marcus glanced down at his open Bible, still resting on his knee. The page had fallen to Matthew 5, and his eyes landed on a verse he had read a hundred times before: "Blessed are the meek, for they will inherit the earth." He looked up at the flags flanking the pulpit—American and Christian, side by side—and then back down at the words in red.

The dissonance was small, barely a whisper, but it was there.

On the drive home, Marcus replayed the sermon in his mind. He thought about the policies Pastor Rick had praised, the language of warfare and conquest, the certainty that God's will and a particular political agenda were one and the same. He thought about the Jesus he had been reading about all week, the one who told his followers to love their enemies, who touched lepers and welcomed outsiders, who refused a crown and chose a cross instead.

And for the first time in a long time, Marcus let himself give voice to what had only been a whisper all morning, a question that would unsettle everything he thought he knew about faith, country, and following Jesus in public life:

*If this is what taking America back for God looks like, does it actually look like Jesus?*

That question—Marcus's question—is the heart of this book. And the tool we will use to answer it is the Jesus Principle: a simple framework rooted in Scripture that helps us see whether our beliefs and actions move toward him or away from him.

# Sunday Morning:
## When Faith Meets Politics in the Pew

Marcus was not alone in his pew that Sunday morning. Across the United States, millions of Christians gather each week in sanctuaries where the line between worship and political mobilization has grown increasingly thin. What happens in these services—the fusion of patriotic fervor, policy prescriptions, and praise—is reshaping both American Christianity and American democracy, and it deserves careful attention from anyone who wants to understand the difference between following Jesus and following a political tribe.

Research from Pew Research Center reveals that while most Americans support church-state separation in principle, significant portions favor government promotion of Christian moral values.[3] Roughly 28 percent of U.S. adults believe the Bible should take precedence over the will of the people when the two conflict, with that number rising to 42 percent among Republicans.[3] This sentiment does not remain abstract; it shows up concretely in Sunday services where pastors frame political engagement as spiritual obedience and national renewal as a divine mandate.

In many evangelical and conservative congregations, worship services increasingly blend spiritual language with explicit political messaging.[1] Pastors affiliated with movements like the New Apostolic Reformation—a network that teaches Christians must take control of society's key institutions through a strategy called the Seven Mountain Mandate—encourage congregants to view themselves as engaged in spiritual warfare for dominance over government, education, media, and family.[1] Flyers appear in church foyers urging Christians to see themselves as "the enemy" in cultural battles.[1] Sermons portray America as a divinely ordained Christian nation under siege from secular forces, and faithful citizenship becomes synonymous with reclaiming political dominance.[1]

The fusion of faith and partisan politics in the pew is not merely rhetorical. Church leaders actively mobilize congregations for local political action, from school board elections to advocacy campaigns against policies they frame as threats to Christian values.[1] In one documented case, three members of LifeGate Church in Pennsylvania won seats on the Elizabethtown School Board in 2021, flipping it to a conservative majority; by June 2025, the board had partnered with a Christian legal organization to implement policies banning transgender athletes from school sports.[1] Pastor Don Lamb, who leads the congregation, follows influential Christian nationalist figures and preaches against what he terms "liberal nationalism," framing local governance as an extension of Sunday worship.[1]

Abby Abildness, a regional leader in the New Apostolic Reformation who works with state legislative prayer caucuses, articulated the strategy plainly: "We need them and they need us, because we can't go write those laws."[1] The collaboration between pastors and legislators blurs the boundary between spiritual authority and civil power, with church services serving as organizing hubs for political campaigns presented as obedience to God's will.

Not all pastors embrace this fusion. Progressive and mainline Christian leaders have begun using their own pulpits to challenge Christian nationalism as a distortion of Jesus' teachings. Pastor Louise Westfall of Central Denver Presbyterian Church warned her congregation that Christian nationalism "threatens to upend the United States Constitution and First Amendment separation of Church and State," pointing to Jesus' exchange with Pilate in which he described his kingdom as "not of this world"—a spiritual reality distinct from earthly government.[2]

The Sunday experience Marcus encountered—where patriotic fervor, policy prescriptions, and worship converge—reflects a broader movement reshaping American Christianity. What happens in the pew on Sunday morning increasingly determines what happens at the ballot box, the school board meeting, and the statehouse. The question forming in Marcus's mind is the question facing millions of Christians in similar pews: when faith and politics meet in worship, which one is shaping the other?

# The Sermon:
## "Taking America Back" as Spiritual Mandate

Pastor Rick's sermon that morning was not an outlier. Across the United States, sermons framing political engagement as spiritual warfare and national reclamation as divine mandate have become increasingly common in evangelical and conservative congregations. This messaging follows a consistent pattern: invoking divine providence and America's supposed Christian founding, portraying the nation as locked in existential conflict between godly order and secular chaos, and presenting "taking America back for God" not as one political opinion among many but as obedience to Scripture itself.[47]

The rhetoric draws on the ideology defined earlier.[4] Sociologist Andrew Whitehead, co-author of *Taking America Back for God*, explains that Christian nationalism "believes that this country was made for and by folks who embrace this particular type of Christianity and that the government should uphold, defend, and institute again this particular expression of Christianity as central to American civic life."[6] This framework turns contested policy positions into tests of loyalty to God, cloaking political goals in religious symbolism so that disagreement feels like disobedience.[4]

When Pastor Rick praised specific legislative agendas from the pulpit—restrictions on reproductive health care, rollbacks of LGBTQ+ protections, tighter immigration enforcement, expanded religious exemptions allowing discrimination—he framed them not as debatable applications of Christian ethics but as "God's blueprint for national renewal." The sermon left no room for faithful disagreement; to question the agenda was to question God himself. This pattern appears in congregations nationwide, where worship services increasingly blend spiritual language with explicit political messaging, and pastors present policy prescriptions as non-negotiable biblical truth.[92]

What makes this kind of messaging effective is its ability to transform political preferences into spiritual mandates. Within this framework, pastors urge congregants to see governance itself as an extension of Sunday worship, and church leaders actively mobilize for local political action—from school board elections to legislative advocacy campaigns—in that same spirit.

Yet as co-author Samuel Perry observes, this ideology "is becoming devoid of any kind of moral content. It is certainly associated with heightened traditional markers of religiosity, and yet it is not necessarily associated with indicators of what you would consider a Christ-like morality: nothing of self-sacrifice, nothing of tolerance, certainly, nothing of loving one's neighbor unless that neighbor is exactly like you."[6] The movement co-opts Christian language for ethno-national power, fostering attitudes that conflict with Jesus' teachings on humility, enemy-love, and sacrificial service.[46]

## Marcus's Question: Does This Look Like Jesus?

Marcus's question—Does this look like Jesus?—is not unique to him. It has quietly troubled millions of Christians sitting in pews where political agendas are baptized as divine mandates. The Jesus invoked from many pulpits bears little resemblance to the Jesus they encounter in Scripture.

**Christian nationalism**, as defined earlier, is an ideology that fuses a particular expression of Christianity with American civic life, treating the nation as if it were made for and by one version of Christianity and insisting that government should uphold, defend, and reinstitute that expression as central to American identity.[8] [10] [11] This ideology emphasizes power, boundaries, and order—manifesting in support for restrictive immigration policies, traditional gender hierarchies, and ethno-national separation—all cloaked in religious symbolism that elevates political goals to transcendent status.

What makes Marcus's question so urgent is that Christian nationalism presents itself not as one political option among many but as biblical obedience itself. When pastors frame specific policy agendas as "God's blueprint for national renewal," they leave no room for faithful disagreement. To question the agenda becomes indistinguishable from questioning God.

Yet the New Testament portrait of Jesus resists this fusion at every turn. When Jesus stands before Pilate, he does not deny being a king but explicitly distances his kingdom from the world's coercive logic: "My Kingdom is not of this world. If my Kingdom were of this world, then my servants would fight, that I wouldn't be delivered to the Jews. But now my Kingdom is not from here" (John 18:36). Jesus refuses the temptation to gain "all the kingdoms of the world" through political shortcuts (Matthew 4:8–10), teaches that greatness means servanthood rather than domination (Matthew 20:25–28), and enters Jerusalem on a donkey rather than with warhorses and chariots. The dominant New Testament pattern is cruciform power—self-emptying, enemy-loving, non-coercive witness—rather than majoritarian control or sacralized violence.[8][10][11]

Marcus's unease grows sharper when he considers the historical fruit of church-state fusion. The execution of Quaker Mary Dyer in 1660 Massachusetts Bay stands as a sobering reminder.[9] Dyer was hanged on Boston Common by Puritan authorities for defying laws banishing Quakers, an act of state violence carried out by a self-consciously Christian commonwealth enforcing religious orthodoxy.[9] On the gallows, when urged to repent and save her life, she replied, "Nay, man, I am not now to repent."[9] Her death was not a pagan atrocity but the logical outcome of empowering the state to enforce doctrinal purity. The logic that killed Dyer is the same logic at work when any government claims divine authorization to punish religious dissent or enforce theological boundaries through civil law.

Marcus's question is therefore not merely political but deeply theological: Is this project forming him—and his nation—into the likeness of Christ, or into the likeness of the powers Jesus unmasked and overcame at the cross? The answer will require him to choose between the political tribe that has shaped his identity and the way of Jesus revealed in Scripture. The tool we will use throughout this book to help answer that question is the Jesus Principle—a simple framework rooted in Jesus' own teaching. It asks whether something bears good fruit, protects the vulnerable, honors the Golden Rule, and tells the truth, and those tests will guide us through every issue this book explores.

Marcus left church that Sunday morning with his Bible under his arm and a question lodged in his chest that he could not shake loose. The sermon had sounded so certain, so righteous, so unmistakably faithful, and yet when he held it up against the red letters in Matthew, something felt off. The Jesus who blessed the meek and commanded enemy-love seemed a long way from the Jesus being invoked to justify immigration raids, abortion bans enforced through criminal prosecution, and laws designed to marginalize LGBTQ+ neighbors. Marcus did not yet have the language to name what troubled him, but he had taken the first step: he had allowed himself to ask whether the political project being preached from his pulpit actually reflected the person and teaching of Jesus Christ.

This opening chapter has introduced the central tension that will drive the entire book. Millions of Christians like Marcus sit in congregations where worship and political mobilization have become indistinguishable, where "taking America back for God" is treated as the only faithful option.

Yet the dissonance Marcus felt is not an accident. It reflects a fundamental conflict between Christian nationalism and the way of Jesus revealed in Scripture. As we saw earlier, Christian nationalism seeks a close fusion between a particular type of Christianity and American civic life, one that emphasizes power, boundaries, and order rather than the self-emptying, non-coercive witness of the Gospels. This ideology is becoming disconnected from Christ-like morality and bearing little resemblance to self-sacrifice, tolerance, or genuine love of neighbor.

The question Marcus asked himself in the parking lot is the question this book will pursue through every chapter. It is a simple question, but it cuts through layers of partisan rhetoric, denominational tradition, and cultural habit to expose what is actually being formed in the lives of believers and in the public square. The chapters ahead will use the Jesus Principle—asking whether any belief or action is moving us toward Jesus or away from him—to evaluate political claims made in Jesus' name. Marcus's journey is just beginning. He does not yet know that the ideology he has absorbed will be tested in every arena he examines, from women's bodies, race, LGBTQ+ youth, law and order, and the fusion of church and state. He does not yet see that following Jesus will require him to choose between the political tribe that has shaped his identity and the way of the cross. But he has taken the first step, and that step is enough.

The question is no longer whether Marcus will ask if this looks like Jesus, but whether he—and readers like him—will have the courage to follow wherever the answer leads.

# CHAPTER 2.

# WHAT IS CHRISTIAN NATIONALISM, REALLY? FAITH, PATRIOTISM, AND THE PURSUIT OF POWER

The coffee in Marcus's hand had gone cold as he sat at his kitchen table, staring at the notes he'd scribbled during last Sunday's sermon. Pastor Rick's words kept echoing—"biblical government," "Christian foundations," "restoring God's order"—but Marcus couldn't shake the feeling that something important was hiding in plain sight, something he'd never thought to question before.

What exactly *was* Christian nationalism, and how was it different from simply being a Christian who loved his country and cared about politics? Marcus had always assumed they were the same thing, that standing up for "biblical values" in the public square was just part of faithful citizenship, no different from his grandparents' generation voting their conscience or his church's long tradition of community service. But the unease that had started in the pew last Sunday refused to fade, and now he found himself asking questions he'd never needed to ask before.

This chapter draws the line that Marcus is beginning to see: between Christian nationalism and authentic Christian faith, between healthy patriotism and the dangerous fusion of religion with political power, between legitimate Christian engagement in democracy and a project that seeks to legally privilege one group's theology while relegating everyone else—including other Christians—to second-class citizenship. These distinctions matter because Christian nationalism wraps itself in the language of faith, flag, and family in ways that make it nearly invisible to those inside the movement, and because failing to see the difference has led millions of sincere believers to support an agenda that, when examined closely, looks less like following Jesus and more like pursuing dominance.

The chapter first helps readers see what Christian nationalism is and how it differs from ordinary Christian political participation. While Christians across the theological spectrum have always engaged in public life—advocating for justice, serving neighbors, and voting according to conscience—Christian nationalism goes further, insisting that America was founded as a Christian nation, that its laws should reflect a particular version of biblical teaching, and that the country's identity and future depend on maintaining a narrow version of Christian cultural and legal control. This ideology treats some citizens as "real Americans" whose faith and heritage give them a privileged claim on the nation, while casting others—religious minorities, the nonreligious, and Christians who read the Bible differently—as threats to be resisted or problems to be managed.

The chapter then tackles the "Christian nation" founding myth head-on, examining what the founders actually said and why historians find the claim misleading. Readers will see that the Constitution mentions God zero times, establishes no religious test for office, and protects religious liberty for all, not because the founders were hostile to faith, but because they had seen the damage done when governments tried to enforce religious uniformity. The evidence reveals a founding generation far more diverse in belief and far more committed to separating church and state than Christian nationalist narratives admit.

By unpacking how Christian nationalism fuses a specific theological and cultural vision with American identity and law, the chapter helps readers recognize the ideology when they encounter it in sermons, slogans, and policy proposals. Marcus begins to see that what he heard as "just what the Bible clearly teaches" is actually part of a larger political project, one that consistently privileges the already powerful, defines belonging in narrow terms, and uses the language of faith to pursue outcomes that often look nothing like the way of Jesus. This chapter lays the foundation for everything that follows. Before readers can evaluate Christian nationalism through the Jesus Principle, they need to see it clearly, stripped of its protective camouflage of patriotism and piety. Once the ideology is named and its core claims examined, the question Marcus asked at the end of chapter one becomes unavoidable: Does this actually look like Jesus?[1]

## Christian Nationalism vs. Christian Faith: Drawing the Line

The distinction between Christian nationalism and Christian faith is not a matter of splitting theological hairs or policing who gets to call themselves Christian. It is a question of what Christianity fundamentally *is* and whether the movement claiming to save America for God actually reflects the way of Jesus or something else entirely.

**Christian nationalism is a political ideology, not a Christian denomination or historic creed.** The Kettering Foundation, summarizing the consensus of contemporary social scientists, defines Christian nationalism as "an ideology that desires a close fusion of a particular expression of Christianity with American civic life" and "demands our government, at all levels, vigorously defend this ideology as central to our national identity, public policy, and social belonging."[12] The Christians Against Christian Nationalism campaign, supported by many U.S. denominations, describes it as "a political ideology that seeks to merge Christian and American identities, distorting both the Christian faith and America's constitutional democracy."[17]

Christian faith, by contrast, centers on the person and work of Jesus Christ—his life, death, and resurrection—and calls believers into a transnational community whose primary citizenship is in heaven, not in any earthly nation. Where Christian nationalism treats America as divinely favored and fuses "God and country" into a quasi-sacred unit,[12] [13] [18] Christian faith insists that God judges every country and cannot be co-opted as the sponsor of one. This is the fundamental line: Christian nationalism makes the nation an object of religious devotion; Christian faith reserves ultimate allegiance for Christ alone.

The ideology reveals itself most clearly in how it answers the question, "Who belongs?"[14] Research shows that Christian nationalism consistently privileges traditional social hierarchies—men over women, heterosexual over LGBTQ+, "traditional" families over others—and defines the ideal American as White and native-born.[12] It builds a narrative in which *this* group "created this country" and thus should retain easier access to civil rights, social benefits, and political power.[12] Christian faith, however, understands the people of God as multiethnic and status-leveling, where distinctions of race, ethnicity, and gender do not determine standing before God or belonging in the community. Any ideology that constructs political belonging around such hierarchies stands in profound tension with the gospel.

**Christian nationalism also differs sharply from healthy patriotism.** Patriotism is grateful, critical love for one's country and a willingness to seek its good while acknowledging its sins. Nationalism, by contrast, insists that one's nation is superior, uniquely chosen, and entitled to dominance. Christian nationalism blends this nationalism with religious language, giving theological backing to national self-exaltation and treating dissent or diversity as threats to a sacred order.

Many Christians across the theological spectrum have always engaged in public life, advocating for justice, serving neighbors, voting according to conscience.[16] That engagement becomes Christian nationalism when Christianity is no longer a moral voice among many but the preferred or imposed civil religion,[15] [17] when belonging and rights in the nation become tied to religious conformity, and when the goal shifts from persuasion within pluralism to legal and cultural control.

The practical test is straightforward. Christian nationalism seeks legal privilege for a particular version of Christianity, often implying that government power should enforce "biblical" morality or Christianity's social dominance.[13] [15] [17] Pew Research has documented that many Americans define Christian nationalism precisely as "imposing Christian beliefs on American citizens" and wanting Christianity to have a "privileged" place in law and policy.[15] Historic Christian theology, however, insists that genuine faith cannot be coerced and that the church's mission is proclamation, service, and sacrificial love, and not control of the state.

Marcus had never thought to ask these questions before. He had assumed that standing up for "biblical values" in the public square was simply faithful citizenship. But now, staring at his notes, he began to see that what he had heard as Christianity shaping politics might actually be politics hijacking Christian symbols, and that the difference mattered more than he ever imagined.

## The "Christian Nation" Myth: What the Founders Actually Said

Marcus had heard the phrase "Christian nation" his entire life—in sermons, on Christian radio, in campaign speeches—and had never questioned it. The story seemed obvious: the Pilgrims came seeking religious freedom, the founders were devout Christians, and the Constitution was built on biblical principles. But when he finally sat down to read what the founders actually wrote, the story he had been told began to unravel.

The United States Constitution, ratified in 1787, contains no reference to Jesus Christ, Christianity, the Bible, or the church.[20] This silence is not an oversight but a deliberate choice. Article VI explicitly states that "no religious Test shall ever be required as a Qualification to any Office or public Trust under the United States," directly rejecting the idea that Christian belief should be a prerequisite for citizenship or leadership.[20] The First Amendment, ratified in 1791, reinforces this framework: "Congress shall make no law respecting an establishment of religion, or prohibiting the free exercise thereof."[20] These provisions establish a government that is religiously neutral in structure, protecting liberty of conscience for all rather than privileging one faith tradition.[20]

The clearest official statement on the matter came just a decade after the Constitution's ratification. In 1797, the Treaty of Tripoli—negotiated under George Washington and unanimously ratified by the Senate under John Adams—declared in Article 11 that "the Government of the United States of America is not, in any sense, founded on the Christian religion."[20] This was not a private opinion or offhand remark but a ratified federal treaty, publicly printed and uncontroversial at the time.[20] The government most closely associated with the founding generation was willing to state, as a matter of international diplomacy, that the United States was not a Christian nation in any legal or covenantal sense.[19]

The founders' personal writings reinforce this constitutional framework. Thomas Jefferson, in his 1802 letter to the Danbury Baptist Association, praised the First Amendment for building "a wall of separation between church and state" and insisted that religion "lies solely between man and his God," beyond the jurisdiction of government.[20] James Madison, often called the Father of the Constitution and primary author of the First Amendment, argued throughout his career that state support of religion corrupts both church and government and that faith must remain a matter of personal conviction, not civil mandate.

George Washington spoke frequently of Providence in generic terms that could be embraced by Christians, deists, and other theists, but his official messages never declared a Christian covenant for the nation.[20] His administration approved the Treaty of Tripoli negotiations, and he consistently avoided sectarian language in public documents.[20] Even John Adams, who valued Christian morality and once wrote that "the general principles on which the fathers achieved independence were the general principles of Christianity," signed the Treaty of Tripoli and supported a Constitution with no reference to biblical authority.[20] [21] Adams' comment is best understood as affirming that revolutionary ideals like equality and human dignity harmonized with Christian

15

ethical teaching, not as a claim that the United States was legally a Christian state.[21]

Historians note that the most influential founders were not a bloc of orthodox evangelicals but a diverse group, many of whom fit the category of "theistic rationalists"—believers in a providential God who nonetheless grounded the republic in natural rights and popular sovereignty rather than biblical covenant or church authority.[19] The distinction matters: America's people were often culturally Christian, but its government was explicitly designed to avoid establishing any religion, Christian or otherwise.[19]

Marcus stared at the Treaty of Tripoli text on his laptop screen, reading the words again: "not, in any sense, founded on the Christian religion." He had never heard this document mentioned at church, never seen it quoted in the Christian media he consumed. The founders he had been told were building a Christian nation had, in their own words and by their own design, done something else entirely, and the gap between the story he had believed and the evidence in front of him was too wide to ignore.

## Power, Belonging, and Who Counts as a "Real American"

Christian nationalism does not merely advocate for Christian values in public life; it constructs a hierarchy of belonging that determines who counts as a legitimate American and who does not. This hierarchy is not incidental to the ideology but central to it, shaping policies and rhetoric that consistently privilege certain groups while marginalizing others.[12] The Kettering Foundation's analysis, summarizing contemporary social science research, identifies this pattern clearly: Christian nationalism "poses a specific threat to democracy as it envisions a very specific preferred citizen who is both White and a natural-born," and "it is this group who should enjoy the easiest access to civil rights, social benefits, and political power."[12]

The ideology builds its vision of belonging on a revisionist historical narrative that credits White Christians with founding the nation and frames their cultural dominance as both natural and divinely ordained.[12][22] This narrative treats America as a Christian nation not only in the sense that many of its people have been Christian, but in the stronger claim that the country was created *by* and *for* Christians—specifically, White Protestant Christians—and that this identity must be preserved through law and policy.[12][13][17][22] Everyone else becomes, at best, a guest in someone else's country, tolerated so long as they do not threaten the cultural and political primacy of the "real Americans."[12][14]

Research consistently shows that Christian nationalism correlates with support for policies that reinforce these boundaries.[12] Those who score higher on measures of Christian nationalist belief are significantly more likely to favor restrictive immigration policies, oppose pathways to citizenship for undocumented immigrants, support aggressive deportation measures, and view refugees and asylum seekers as threats rather than neighbors in need.[12][22] The same pattern appears in attitudes toward voting rights, where Christian nationalism predicts support for measures that make voting more difficult—measures that disproportionately affect Black, Latino, and low-income citizens.[12] The ideology frames these restrictions not as voter suppression but as protecting the integrity of elections from people who do not fully belong.[12]

Political scientist Eric L. McDaniel of the University of Texas at Austin describes Christian nationalism as "a worldview that guides how people believe the nation should be structured and who belongs there."[14] This worldview extends beyond questions of immigration and voting to encompass the full range of social policy. Christian nationalism envisions traditional hierarchies—men over women, heterosexual families over all others, native-born over immigrant—as essential to national strength and divine order.[12] Diversity, whether racial, ethnic, or religious, is perceived not as a source of richness but as a threat to cohesion and identity.[12][17][23]

The Christians Against Christian Nationalism coalition, supported by numerous denominations and faith leaders, warns that this ideology "inspires acts of violence and intimidation, including vandalism, bomb threats, arson, hate crimes, and attacks on houses of worship."[23] When belonging is defined so narrowly and power is understood as a zero-sum contest, those who fall outside the boundaries become not merely political opponents but existential threats to the nation's identity and survival.[12]

Marcus had never thought of himself as someone who believed in second-class citizenship. He had Black colleagues, his church's worship team was diverse, and he genuinely believed in equal rights under the law. But as he listened more carefully to the language around him—the casual references to "real Americans," the warnings about immigrants "changing our country," the insistence that certain people were "more American" than others—he began to see a pattern he had never noticed before. The ideology he had absorbed did not explicitly say that some people mattered less; it simply built a world in which some people's rights, safety, and dignity were always negotiable while others never were. And once he saw it, he could not unsee it. Marcus closed his notebook and stared out the kitchen window at the flag hanging from his neighbor's porch, the same flag he had saluted at church picnics and political rallies for as long as he could remember. For the first time in his life, he found himself asking whether loving that flag and following Jesus were actually the same thing, or whether he had been taught to confuse the two so thoroughly that he could no longer tell them apart.

The evidence laid out in this chapter draws a clear line that millions of sincere Christians have rarely been invited to see. **Christian nationalism is not synonymous with Christian faith, healthy patriotism, or faithful political engagement.** It is a political ideology that fuses a particular, usually fundamentalist, expression of Christianity with American identity and law, demanding that government defend this fusion as central to national belonging and public policy. Where Christian faith centers on Jesus Christ and calls believers into a transnational community whose ultimate citizenship is in heaven, Christian nationalism treats America as divinely favored and makes the nation itself an object of religious devotion. The distinction is not semantic; it is the difference between following Jesus and conscripting him into service of a political project.

The historical record exposes the "Christian nation" founding myth as revisionist storytelling rather than constitutional fact. The founders designed a government with no religious test for office and explicit protections for religious liberty that apply equally to all. The Treaty of Tripoli, ratified unanimously by the founding generation's Senate, declared in plain language that "the Government of the United States of America is not, in any sense, founded on the Christian religion." This was not an accident or oversight but a deliberate choice to build a republic on popular sovereignty and natural rights rather than biblical covenant or ecclesiastical authority. The gap between what the founders actually said and what Christian nationalist narratives claim they said is too wide to be bridged by selective quotation or wishful thinking.

**Most troubling is the way Christian nationalism constructs a hierarchy of belonging that determines who counts as a "real American" and who does not.** Research shows that the ideology consistently privileges White, native-born Christians as the rightful owners of the nation, while pushing others to the margins of civic life. This hierarchy is not incidental but central, shaping policies on immigration, voting rights, policing, and social services in ways that systematically disadvantage Black, Latino, and immigrant communities. When belonging is defined so narrowly and power is understood as a zero-sum contest, diversity becomes a threat rather than a gift, and neighbors become enemies to be controlled rather than fellow image-bearers to be loved.

Marcus had never set out to support second-class citizenship or to wrap political power in the language of faith. He had simply absorbed the story he was told—that standing up for "biblical values" and "taking America back for God" were the same as faithful discipleship. But now, with the founders' own words in front of him and the real-world consequences of Christian nationalist policies becoming impossible to ignore, he could see that the ideology he had embraced was not leading him closer to Jesus but further away.

The question that began in the pew last Sunday had grown sharper and more urgent: If this is what taking America back for God looks like, does it actually look like Jesus? Marcus did not yet have all the answers, but he knew he needed a better compass, one that could cut through the slogans, test the claims, and help him follow Jesus rather than a political tribe. He was ready to find it.

# CHAPTER 3.

# THE JESUS PRINCIPLE: A BETTER COMPASS FOR NAVIGATING FAITH IN POLITICS

On one page, a pastor had quoted Romans 13 to argue that Christians must support every government action without question. On the facing page, another leader had cited the same chapter to justify civil disobedience against policies he deemed ungodly. One column listed verses used to prove that caring for the poor meant expanding government assistance; another column held verses deployed to argue that such programs violated biblical principles of personal responsibility. The same Bible, the same Jesus, but completely opposite conclusions about what faithfulness required in the public square.

Marcus closed the notebook and rubbed his eyes. If everyone claimed to be following Scripture, how was he supposed to know which voice to trust? More importantly, how could he be sure that his own convictions—the ones he'd held for decades and never thought to question—were actually rooted in Jesus rather than just in the political tribe he'd always belonged to?

The question that had been nagging at him since that Sunday morning sermon had sharpened into something more urgent: he needed a way to tell the difference between following Jesus and following a political agenda dressed up in religious language. He needed a compass, a filter, something simple enough to remember in the voting booth and the church lobby but robust enough to cut through the fog of conflicting claims made in God's name.

What Marcus didn't yet know was that Jesus and the Apostle Paul had already provided exactly that kind of compass. This chapter introduces what we'll call **the Jesus Principle**: a simple framework that any Christian can use to evaluate political claims made in Jesus' name. The Jesus Principle asks one straightforward question: **Are your beliefs and actions moving toward the character and teachings of Jesus, or farther away from them?** It then uses four questions to help you discern that direction in real-world choices:

*Does it bear the fruit of the Spirit?* Does the policy or rhetoric produce love, joy, peace, patience, kindness, goodness, faithfulness, gentleness, and self-control—or does it generate fear, division, cruelty, and harm?

*Does it care for the vulnerable?* Does it protect and uplift "the least of these"—the poor, the sick, the stranger, the marginalized—or does it sacrifice them for the comfort and power of those already secure?

*Would I want this done to me or to those I love?* Does it pass the Golden Rule test when we imagine ourselves or our own families on the receiving end?

*Is it true?* Does it align with the actual life and teaching of Jesus, and does it rely on facts rather than fear, distortion, or outright falsehood?

Each of these four questions form a reliable test for distinguishing authentic discipleship from ideology wrapped in Scripture. Readers who want a fuller biblical and practical exploration of these four questions can find it in my first book, *The Jesus Principle*, which develops this framework in depth and applies it to a wide range of issues.

After explaining each question and grounding it in the Gospels, we'll test-drive the framework on two concrete issues that touch every American life: immigration policy and health care access. Without diving into partisan policy weeds, we'll probe whether the rhetoric and proposals we hear in church lobbies and campaign rallies actually move us toward Jesus or away from him.

By the end of this chapter, Marcus—and every reader—will have a tool to carry into every election season, every sermon, and every family argument about faith and politics. More importantly, they'll have begun the work of disentangling Jesus from tribe and following the Teacher rather than the team.

## The Four Questions:
## A Framework Rooted in the New Testament

The framework Marcus needed was not something new or invented. It had been present in Jesus' and Paul's teaching all along, woven through the Gospels and New Testament in ways that made it accessible to fishermen and tax collectors, children and scholars alike. What Marcus was searching for—a reliable compass to navigate the conflicting political claims made in Jesus' name—already existed.

**Does it bear the fruit of the Spirit?** This first question comes from Galatians 5:22–23, where Paul describes the observable outcomes of a life shaped by Jesus and the Holy Spirit: love, joy, peace, patience, kindness, goodness, faithfulness, gentleness, and self-control. Jesus taught that trees are known by their fruit, warning that false prophets can be recognized not by their claims, but by what they actually produce. When a political claim is made in Jesus' name, this question asks what kind of fruit it bears in real people's lives. If a policy produces fear and cruelty rather than love and gentleness, it points away from Jesus, not toward him.

**Does it care for the vulnerable?** Throughout the Gospels, Jesus consistently identified himself with "the least of these"—the poor, the sick, the hungry, the stranger, and the prisoner. In Matthew 25, he made clear that how his followers treat the most vulnerable is how they treat him. This question asks whether a policy or position protects those with the least power and security, or whether it sacrifices them for the advantage of those already comfortable. Any agenda that harms the vulnerable while claiming to follow Jesus moves away from his character and teaching, regardless of how many Bible verses are cited in its defense.

**Would I want this done to me or to those I love?** Jesus called this the Golden Rule, and he taught it as the summation of the Law and the Prophets. In Matthew 7:12, he instructed his followers to do to others what they would want done to themselves. This question personalizes every political position by asking how it would feel from the receiving end. It cuts through abstraction by inviting people to imagine their own children, parents, or neighbors subjected to the policy being debated. If the answer is no—if we would not accept this treatment for our own loved ones—then the position moves us away from Jesus, not toward him.

**Is it true?** Jesus described himself as the way, the truth, and the life, and he promised that the truth would set people free. This last question asks whether a claim aligns with the actual life and teaching of Jesus as recorded in the Gospels, and whether it relies on facts rather than fear or falsehood.[25] It requires checking political rhetoric against Scripture in context, not isolated proof texts, and it demands honesty about real-world evidence. Truth-telling is not optional in Christian discipleship; it is foundational. When claims distort Jesus' teaching or rely on misinformation, they move us away from him.

These four questions work together as tools for discernment, helping us answer the core question at every turn: toward Jesus, or away from him?[24]

## Test Drive:
## Immigration and the Fruit of Compassion

With the four questions of the Jesus Principle now in hand, Marcus needed to see how they worked in practice. The first test case arrived unexpectedly during a Wednesday night church meeting, when a deacon stood to announce that ICE had detained the father of three children in the youth group. The family had been part of the congregation for eight years. The children were U.S. citizens; their father had overstayed a visa decades earlier and was now facing deportation. Some members immediately called for the church to help. Others insisted that "illegal is illegal" and quoted Romans 13 about obeying government authorities. Both sides claimed Scripture, but

Marcus now had a framework to cut through the competing claims by asking the core question: does this move us toward Jesus or away from him?

The first question asked whether the policy bears the fruit of the Spirit. Nations do have a legitimate responsibility to set and enforce borders; Scripture doesn't require governments to ignore laws or abandon prudential judgment about migration. But research shows that aggressive immigration enforcement—including workplace raids, family separation, and prolonged detention—produces measurable trauma in children, even those who are U.S. citizens. Studies document increased anxiety, depression, and fear of going to school among children whose parents face deportation. Communities experience heightened distrust of law enforcement, making residents less likely to report crimes or seek help. These outcomes—fear, trauma, fractured families, and children living in constant terror—look nothing like the fruit of love, peace, and gentleness that Paul describes in Galatians. When policies produce such harm, especially to children, they point away from Jesus, not toward him."

The second question focused Marcus's attention on the vulnerable. Throughout the Gospels, Jesus consistently identified himself with the stranger and the marginalized. In Matthew 25, he declared that how his followers treat "the least of these" is how they treat him.[26] The Hebrew Scriptures command God's people repeatedly to care for the foreigner and the sojourner, reminding Israel that they themselves were once strangers in Egypt. Immigration policy that treats asylum seekers with cruelty, separates parents from children, or denies due process to those fleeing violence fails the test of caring for those Jesus called "the least of these," regardless of how many times Romans 13 is quoted in its defense.

The Golden Rule brought the issue into sharper focus. Marcus imagined his own grandchildren growing up in a country torn by gang violence or economic collapse, his daughter making the desperate choice to seek safety elsewhere, his family arriving at a border and being met with detention, separation, or immediate deportation without a hearing. Would he want a system that treated his loved ones as criminals for seeking refuge? Protecting a border is one thing; dehumanizing those who cross it is another. Would he accept rhetoric that dehumanized them as "invaders" or "illegals?" The question answered itself. If he would not accept such treatment for his own family, supporting policies that impose it on other families violated the command to do unto others as he would have them do unto him.

The last question demanded truthfulness. Marcus had heard repeatedly that immigrants were dangerous criminals and that the Bible commands absolute obedience to government immigration law. But when he examined the evidence, he found a different picture. Research consistently shows that immigrants—including undocumented immigrants—commit crimes at lower rates than native-born citizens. And a fuller reading of Scripture reveals that the same apostle Paul who wrote Romans 13 also defied unjust laws when they conflicted with God's commands, and that the early church regularly practiced civil disobedience. Claims that equate harsh, indiscriminate immigration crackdowns with God's will ignore both the facts and the witness of Scripture itself.

By the time Marcus finished walking through the four questions, his direction was unmistakable. Policies that produce trauma in children, harm vulnerable families seeking safety, fail the Golden Rule test, and rely on distorted facts move us away from Jesus, not toward him. The Jesus Principle had given him a compass that worked.

## Test Drive:
## Health Care Access and the Golden Rule

Marcus had watched the four questions cut through the fog around immigration, but he needed to see whether the framework held up when the stakes felt even more personal. The second test case arrived unbidden: his church's small group had spent an entire evening debating whether Christians should support efforts to expand health insurance coverage or whether such programs represented government overreach that violated biblical principles of self-reliance. The conversation had grown heated, with Scripture cited on both sides, and Marcus had left feeling more confused than convicted. Now, with the Jesus Principle in hand, he returned to the question: did expanding access to health care move us toward Jesus or away from him?

## The Golden Rule as the Entry Point

The Golden Rule offered the most direct path into the health care debate.[29][30] Jesus had commanded his followers to do to others what they would want done to themselves, and Marcus found that this question became uncomfortably concrete when applied to medical access. He imagined his own family facing a cancer diagnosis without insurance, or his grandchildren denied treatment for a chronic condition because their parents earned too little to afford coverage but too much to qualify for assistance. Would he want a system that left his loved ones choosing between bankruptcy and untreated illness? Would he accept emergency rooms as the only option for his daughter's diabetes care, or his aging mother turned away from a specialist because she lacked the right coverage? The answer was immediate and unambiguous. If he would not accept such treatment for his own family, supporting policies that imposed it on millions of other families violated the command Jesus had called the summation of the Law and the Prophets. On this measure alone, restricting health care access moved us away from Jesus, not toward him.[29][33]

## Care for the Vulnerable

The question of care for the vulnerable sharpened the analysis further. Research from the Kaiser Family Foundation shows that before the Affordable Care Act's Medicaid expansion, millions of low-income adults fell into a coverage gap, earning too much for traditional Medicaid but too little to afford private insurance.[30][34] States that refused to expand Medicaid left disproportionate numbers of Black and Hispanic residents uninsured, and rural hospitals serving these populations faced closure at alarming rates.[30][34] Jesus had identified himself with the sick in Matthew 25, declaring that how his followers treat those without health is how they treat him. Any policy framework that increases the number of people unable to access care—particularly among communities already facing systemic disadvantage—fails the test of protecting those Jesus called "the least of these," regardless of how it is justified through appeals to market principles or limited government.[29][31] By this measure, policies that widen coverage gaps move us away from Jesus's character and teaching.

## The Fruit Test

The fruit test showed that results didn't line up with the claims of compassion. Studies published in medical journals document that lack of insurance coverage is associated with delayed diagnosis, worse health outcomes, and tens of thousands of preventable deaths annually.[32] Families facing medical bankruptcy experience cascading harms: housing instability, food insecurity, and long-term economic damage that affects children's educational attainment and future opportunity. These outcomes—increased suffering, preventable death, multigenerational poverty—bear no resemblance to the fruit of love, peace, or goodness that Paul describes in Galatians.

## The Truth Test

The truth question demanded honesty about both Scripture and evidence. Marcus had repeatedly heard that Jesus never advocated for government programs and that charity should remain private, but when he read the Gospels carefully, he found a Jesus who healed without asking about worthiness or ability to pay, who fed crowds without means-testing, and who commanded his followers to care for the sick as a non-negotiable mark of discipleship.[29][33] The claim that private charity could replace systemic health coverage ignored the scale: even the most generous churches and nonprofits lack the resources to provide comprehensive medical care for tens of millions of uninsured Americans, and data show that when public coverage contracts, private charity cannot fill the gap.[30][31]

By the time Marcus finished walking through the four questions, the path had become clear. Policies that fail the Golden Rule, harm the vulnerable, produce bad fruit, and rely on selective readings of Scripture move us away from Jesus, not toward him.[29][31][32]

The two test drives—immigration enforcement and health care access—had shown Marcus something he could no longer unsee: the Jesus Principle was not a theoretical exercise but a practical compass that worked in the real world. When he asked whether policies moved him toward the character and teachings of Jesus or farther away, the four questions cut through partisan fog and competing Bible verses to reveal outcomes that either reflected Jesus' character or contradicted it. Policies that produced trauma in children, denied care to the sick, failed the Golden Rule when he imagined his own family on the receiving end, and relied on distorted facts or selective Scripture pointed away from Jesus, not toward him. The framework worked precisely because it forced him to look at actual fruit rather than intentions, to center those most affected rather than those most comfortable, and to measure every claim against the life and teaching of Jesus rather than against party platforms or culture-war battle lines.

What unsettled Marcus most was the recognition that this compass would require him to reassess not just a few hot-button issues but his entire approach to deciding what counted as "Christian" in public life. He had spent decades assuming that the political positions he heard at church were simply what the Bible taught, that faithfulness meant supporting the candidates and policies his pastor endorsed, and that questioning those alignments meant questioning his faith itself. The Jesus Principle revealed a different path: one that measured every claim against Jesus rather than against the loudest voices or the most Scripture citations. It gave him permission to notice contradictions he had been trained to ignore—the same Bible used to justify opposite positions, leaders citing Jesus to defend policies that produced measurable harm to vulnerable neighbors, and rhetoric that failed every test Jesus had given for recognizing his kingdom.

Marcus understood that using this compass consistently would cost him something. It would mean disappointing people in his church who expected political uniformity, risking relationships with friends who saw any deviation from the party line as compromise, and admitting that he had supported policies and rhetoric that did not move toward Jesus. But the alternative—continuing to baptize political tribalism with Jesus' name while ignoring the fruit it produced in real lives—had become impossible. He had seen too much, asked too many questions, and recognized too clearly that the Jesus he met in the Gospels looked nothing like the strongman politics and culture-war dominance he had been told represented God's plan for America.

The Jesus Principle was not the end of Marcus's journey but the beginning of a new way of walking through the world. Christian nationalism claims to speak for Jesus in public life; the Jesus Principle tests whether its policies actually move us toward him or away from him. In the chapters ahead, this same compass will apply to the specific arenas where Christian nationalism has fused faith with power: the debates over whose Bible would rule, the politics of women's bodies, the racial hierarchies embedded in "real American" rhetoric, the treatment of LGBTQ+ youth, the law-and-order promises built on fear, and the threat to soul freedom itself. Each arena will test whether Marcus—and every reader—will choose Jesus over tribe, even when that choice demands letting go of certainties held for an entire lifetime and standing with those the tribe has pushed to the margins.

# CHAPTER 4.

# DUELING BIBLES: WHOSE "BIBLICAL" TRUTH WOULD RULE A CHRISTIAN NATION?

The text message from his daughter arrived while Marcus was reading through Galatians, and it stopped him mid-verse: "Dad, why does Pastor Rick say women can't be elders when Mom's church has had women pastors for thirty years, and they use the same Bible?" He stared at the screen, then at the open page in front of him, suddenly aware that the black-and-white clarity he'd always assumed was there had never really existed. For weeks now, Marcus had been testing the political claims he heard at church against the Jesus Principle. One pattern kept emerging: nearly every argument ended with "the Bible clearly says" or "Scripture is unambiguous"—yet when he actually looked, the clarity vanished the moment he stepped outside his own tradition's reading.

His daughter's question exposed a fault line Marcus had never noticed before. Her mother's Presbyterian church and his own Baptist congregation both claimed to be "Bible -believing," affirmed the authority of Scripture, and insisted they were simply following what God's Word taught. Yet on women in leadership, they reached opposite conclusions. One tradition saw Galatians 3:28—"There is neither Jew nor Greek, there is neither slave nor free man, there is neither male nor female; for you are all one in Christ Jesus."—as the controlling principle and read Paul's restrictive-sounding passages as specific to particular first-century contexts. The other elevated 1

Timothy 2:12—"But I don't permit a woman to teach, nor to exercise authority over a man"—as the timeless rule and treated egalitarian readings as compromise with culture. Both sides could marshal Greek grammar, historical context, and theological arguments. Both accused the other of bending Scripture to fit an agenda. And both were filled with sincere, committed Christians who loved Jesus and believed they were being faithful.

This was not an abstract problem. It was the problem at the heart of every Christian nationalist claim that America should be governed by "biblical law" or that policies should reflect "what the Bible teaches." If two churches in the same town could not agree on whether women could preach, how could a nation of 330 million people—representing tens of thousands of Christian denominations and independent churches, plus Jews, Muslims, Hindus, Buddhists, agnostics, atheists, and everyone in between—ever be governed by a single "biblical" standard? And more urgently, who would decide which interpretation became law?

Marcus was beginning to realize that when Christian nationalists said, "The Bible is clear and easy to understand," they almost always meant "our tradition's reading is clear and easy to understand"—and they wanted the power of the state to enforce that reading on everyone else. The move was subtle but unmistakable: take one faction's interpretation, strip away the centuries of debate and the diversity of faithful disagreement and present it as the only legitimate Christian position. Then demand that the government enshrine it in law, fund it with tax dollars, and punish dissenters. The result was not faithfulness to Scripture but the use of Scripture as a weapon to secure cultural dominance for one group while silencing everyone else.

This chapter exposes that core flaw by walking through three concrete cases where Christians read the same Bible and reach opposite conclusions: the role of women in church and society, the meaning of Romans 13 and the Christian's relationship to civil authority, and the requirements of religious liberty in a pluralistic democracy. In each case, the "dueling Bibles" problem shows that there is no single "biblical" answer the state can enforce without choosing sides in an intra-Christian debate, a choice that always privileges the powerful and harms the vulnerable. By the end, Marcus will see that the Jesus Principle offers a better way: instead of asking "What does *my* tradition say the Bible says?" he must ask whether a policy bears good fruit, protects the vulnerable, honors the Golden Rule, and aligns with truth. That test will show why empowering government to enforce one group's biblical interpretation is not faithfulness but coercion, and why Christians who want to follow Jesus must resist the temptation to turn Caesar into a theologian.

## The Illusion of One "Biblical" View: 45,000 Denominations and Counting

The claim that the Bible clearly teaches a single position on any contested issue runs headlong into an inconvenient fact: Christianity has never agreed on what the Bible clearly teaches. Researchers at the Center for the Study of Global Christianity at Gordon-Conwell Theological Seminary estimate that there are approximately **47,300 Christian denominations and ecclesiastical bodies** worldwide as of mid-2023, with projections reaching 49,000 by 2025 and 64,000 by 2050.[35] These are not minor variations in worship style or organizational structure; they represent fundamental disagreements over doctrine, practice, authority, and ethics, all claimed to be grounded in faithful biblical interpretation.[35][38]

This staggering diversity is not a modern anomaly. Christianity has been fragmenting since its earliest centuries, but the pace accelerated dramatically after the Protestant Reformation introduced the principle of *sola scriptura*—Scripture alone as the ultimate authority.[35][37] That principle, intended to liberate believers from corrupt ecclesiastical hierarchies, also empowered every congregation, pastor, and individual reader to interpret the Bible independently. The result has been exponential division.[35] Protestantism alone now encompasses hundreds of distinct traditions, from Baptists and Methodists to Pentecostals and non-denominational independents, each reading the same Bible and reaching different conclusions about salvation, baptism, church governance, the role of women, the end times, and the Christian's relationship to civil authority.[37]

The numbers tell the story. The World Christian Database, maintained by the Center for the Study of Global Christianity, documents that denominational growth has matched or exceeded overall Christian population growth since 1900.[35] While Christianity claims approximately 2.3 to 2.6 billion adherents globally—making it the world's largest religion—no single denomination commands a majority.[36] Roman Catholicism is the largest single group at roughly 1.3 to 1.4 billion members, yet it represents only about half of all Christians.[36][37][39] The other half is divided among Eastern Orthodox communions (approximately 168 million), historic Protestant denominations (629 million), independent Pentecostal and charismatic movements (409 million), and thousands of smaller groups.[37][39] Even within Catholicism, Eastern Catholic Churches maintain distinct rites and theological emphases, and independent Catholic groups operate outside Vatican authority.[37]

This fragmentation is most pronounced in the Global South, where Christianity is growing fastest.[35] Africa alone is projected to have 754 million Christians by 2025, with rapid proliferation of independent churches and Indigenous denominations that blend biblical interpretation with local cultural contexts.[35] Asia, home to an estimated 417 million Christians, shows similar patterns.[35] Each of these communities claims to be following Scripture faithfully, yet their "biblical" conclusions on everything from polygamy to political resistance vary widely.

The implications for Christian nationalism are devastating. If tens of thousands of denominations cannot agree on whether women may preach, whether baptism requires immersion, or whether Christians may divorce, how can a nation of 330 million people—including not only Christians of every stripe but also Jews, Muslims, Hindus, Buddhists, agnostics, atheists, and adherents of hundreds of other traditions—be governed by "biblical law?"[35][38] Which denomination's Bible would rule? Which version of biblical inerrancy should win out? Would it be the Southern Baptist reading that reserves pastoral leadership for men, or the Presbyterian interpretation that ordains women? The Pentecostal view that emphasizes direct revelation and spiritual gifts, or the Reformed tradition that prioritizes systematic theology and confessional standards? The Anabaptist commitment to pacifism and separation from state power, or the magisterial Protestant embrace of Christian magistrates enforcing divine law? And even among churches that affirm LGBTQ+ dignity, would the state enforce the Episcopal and mainline practice of ordaining gay ministers, the more limited stance of blessing same-sex unions but not performing weddings, or the conservative position that forbids both?

Christian nationalists rarely acknowledge this problem. Instead, they present their own tradition's interpretation as "what the Bible teaches," erasing centuries of faithful disagreement and the lived reality of millions of Christians who read Scripture differently. That erasure is not accidental. It is the necessary move to justify using state power to enforce one faction's theology on everyone else.[35][38]

## Case Studies in Dueling Interpretations: Women, Authority, and the State

The question of women's authority in church and society offers one of the clearest examples of how Christians reading the same Bible reach opposite conclusions and why empowering the state to enforce one interpretation would privilege some believers while silencing others.[39]

### Complementarian vs. Egalitarian: Two Readings, One Scripture

Complementarian Christians, including many Southern Baptists and conservative evangelicals, teach that God designed men and women for distinct, non-interchangeable roles. They point to 1 Timothy 2:12—"But I don't permit a woman to teach, nor to exercise authority over a man, but to be in quietness"—and argue that male headship in home and church reflects the created order.[40] The Southern Baptist Convention's 2000 Baptist Faith and Message declares that "the office of pastor is limited to men as qualified by Scripture," and many complementarian churches extend this principle to argue that women should not hold civil authority either. Pastor Joel Webbon, a Christian nationalist leader, has explicitly called for repealing the Nineteenth Amendment, which granted women the right to vote, arguing that Scripture prevents women from governing.[40]

Egalitarian Christians, by contrast, read the same texts and conclude that gender hierarchy was a cultural accommodation, not God's timeless design. They highlight Galatians 3:28—"There is neither Jew nor Greek, there is neither slave nor free man, there is neither male nor female; for you are all one in Christ Jesus."—as the controlling principle. They note that the New Testament records women serving as prophets, deacons, and co-workers in ministry, including Phoebe (a deacon), Priscilla (who taught Apollos), and Junia (called "outstanding among the apostles" in Romans 16:7).[40] Egalitarians argue that Paul's restrictive instructions addressed specific local problems in Ephesus and Corinth, not universal mandates, and that the early church's later suppression of women's leadership reflected Roman patriarchal norms absorbed over centuries, not Jesus' original vision.[40][43]

Both traditions claim to be "Bible-believing" and include scholars with deep love for Scripture, yet they reach opposite conclusions about whether a woman may preach, vote, or hold public office.

## The State Cannot Adjudicate Theology Without Choosing Sides

This disagreement is not academic. When Christian nationalists demand that government reflect "biblical values" on gender, they are asking the state to take sides in an intra-Christian debate that has divided believers for centuries. If the United States were to become the "Christian nation" that Pastor Rick and others envision, whose interpretation would govern? Would women be barred from elected office, as Webbon advocates, or would they serve as equals, as egalitarian traditions affirm?[40] Would public schools teach complementarian gender roles as divine mandate, or would they honor the convictions of Christians who read Scripture differently?

The answer reveals the authoritarian core of Christian nationalism: the version that wins is always the version held by those with the most political power. In practice, this means that conservative evangelical readings—shaped by twentieth-century reactions against feminism and rooted in particular cultural anxieties—would be enshrined in law and imposed on millions of Christians who interpret the Bible differently, not to mention Jews, Muslims, Hindus, Buddhists, atheists, and others who do not regard the Bible as authoritative at all.[41] [45]

Survey data from the Public Religion Research Institute confirms that Christian nationalism correlates strongly with support for male headship and opposition to women's equality.[42] [44] Sixty-nine percent of Christian nationalism adherents agree that "in a truly Christian family, the husband is the head of the household, and his wife submits to his leadership," and similar majorities believe society has become "too soft and feminine."[42] These convictions shape policy preferences on everything from reproductive rights to workplace protections, with the state deployed to enforce one faction's theology on everyone else.[41] [44]

Marcus had never thought about the women in his own church who felt called to ministry but were told their gifts could only be exercised in children's programs or women's Bible studies. He had never asked what it would mean for his daughter—a lawyer and a believer—to live under laws that treated her as less than fully human because of her gender. Now, reading his daughter's text message again, he realized that "the Bible clearly says" was not a neutral claim but a power move, and the state had no business deciding which Christians were reading Scripture correctly.

## The Jesus Principle Test: Why State-Enforced "Biblical Law" Fails on All Four Counts

Marcus had spent his whole life hearing that America needed to return to "biblical law," but he had never stopped to ask what would happen if the government actually tried to enforce it. Now, sitting with his notebook and the Jesus Principle questions written across the top of the page, he realized that state-enforced "biblical law" would fail every single test Jesus gave for recognizing authentic discipleship.

### Does It Bear the Fruit of the Spirit?

When government power is deployed to enforce religious doctrine, the fruit is not love, joy, peace, patience, kindness, goodness, faithfulness, gentleness, or self-control. History shows that state-enforced religion produces coercion, resentment, hypocrisy, and persecution. The

European wars of religion after the Reformation—when Protestant and Catholic princes used state power to enforce their interpretations of Scripture—killed millions and devastated entire regions.[32] The Puritan experiments in colonial New England, which punished Quakers, banished dissenters, and executed accused witches in the name of biblical law, became cautionary tales of what happens when civil magistrates claim authority over souls.[32]

Even when state enforcement does not produce outright violence, it corrupts both faith and politics. Forced compliance creates shallow, resentful "conversions" rather than genuine transformation. It turns pastors into enforcers and neighbors into informants. It replaces the Spirit's work of conviction and regeneration with the state's tools of fines, imprisonment, and social exclusion. The fruit of such systems is fear, division, and the hollowing out of authentic faith—the opposite of what Galatians 5:22–23 describes.

### Does It Care for the Vulnerable?

State-enforced biblical law inevitably harms the vulnerable because it empowers the majority to define orthodoxy and punish dissenters. [43] In a nation where tens of thousands of Christian denominations and independent churches disagree on fundamental questions of doctrine and practice, any attempt to make one interpretation legally binding will privilege the powerful and marginalize everyone else. Religious minorities—Jews, Muslims, Hindus, Buddhists, Sikhs, and others—become second-class citizens whose beliefs are tolerated at best and criminalized at worst. Christians who read Scripture differently from the ruling faction face legal penalties for their convictions. Atheists and agnostics are excluded from full participation in civic life.

The pattern repeats across history: when the state enforces religious law, the people who suffer most are the poor, the foreign-born, women, racial and sexual minorities, and theological dissenters. Those with wealth, political connections, and cultural capital can navigate or escape enforcement; those without such resources cannot. Jesus consistently stood with the vulnerable against religious and political authorities who used law to control and exclude. State-enforced "biblical law" does the opposite.

## Would I Want This Done to Me?

Marcus tried to imagine his own faith under another religion's legal control. What if Muslims held political power and used the state to enforce Sharia law, requiring all Americans to follow Islamic dietary restrictions, prayer times, and dress codes? What if Hindus mandated vegetarianism and cow protection as civil law? What if atheists banned religious education and church attendance for anyone under eighteen? The thought made his stomach turn, and not because those faiths and atheists are wrong to hold their convictions, but because no one should have the power to use government force to impose their theology on others.

The Golden Rule exposes the authoritarian core of Christian nationalism: those who demand state enforcement of their biblical interpretation would never accept the same treatment from another group. That double standard reveals that the goal is not faithfulness but dominance.

## Is It True to Jesus' Teaching and Example?

Jesus never asked Caesar to enforce discipleship. He refused political power repeatedly, taught that his kingdom was "not of this world," and insisted that faith must be voluntary or it is not faith at all.[32] He rebuked the Pharisees for using religious law to control others while neglecting justice, mercy, and faithfulness.[32] He welcomed outsiders, ate with sinners, and reserved his harshest words for religious leaders who laid heavy burdens on people's shoulders.[32]

State-enforced biblical law fails the Jesus test on every count because it replaces the way of Jesus with the way of Caesar, trading persuasion for coercion and love for control. Marcus closed his Bible and sat in silence, his daughter's question still glowing on his phone's screen. For the first time in his life, he understood that "the Bible clearly says" was not a statement of fact but a claim to power, and that when Christian nationalists demanded government enforce "biblical law," they were not asking the state to honor Scripture but to choose sides in arguments that had divided faithful Christians for two thousand years.

By the time Marcus closed his Bible, he had watched three arenas where sincere believers read the same Bible and reached opposite conclusions: whether women may lead in church and society, how Christians should relate to civil authority, and what religious liberty requires in a diverse democracy. In every case, the "dueling Bibles" problem exposed the same flaw: any "biblical" standard the state enforces will privilege one faction's interpretation and silence all others. When Pastor Rick declared that America must return to biblical government, he was not calling the nation back to Jesus but into a system where his tradition's reading would be written into law and imposed on millions who read Scripture differently, or who did not regard the Bible as authoritative at all.

The Jesus Principle made the problem inescapable: state-enforced "biblical law" fails the fruit, vulnerable, Golden Rule, and truth tests all at once.

Marcus realized that the question his daughter had asked—why two Bible-believing churches could reach opposite conclusions about women in leadership—was the same question that unraveled every Christian nationalist claim. If Baptists and Presbyterians could not agree on whether women may preach, how could our entire nation be governed by a single "biblical" standard? If researchers counted nearly fifty thousand Christian denominations and independent churches worldwide, each claiming to follow Scripture faithfully, whose interpretation would rule? The answer was always the same: the interpretation held by those with the most political power. That was not faithfulness. That was domination dressed in religious language.

The chapter's central insight was this: Christians who want to follow Jesus must stop asking "What does *my* tradition say the Bible says?" and start asking whether a policy bears good fruit, protects the vulnerable, honors the Golden Rule, and aligns with truth. Those four questions cut through the fog of competing biblical claims and expose what is actually at stake. They reveal that Christian nationalism is not about honoring Scripture but about using Scripture as a weapon to secure cultural control for one group while silencing everyone else.

Marcus thought again about the women in his church who had been told their gifts were too dangerous to use, about his daughter practicing law in a world that wanted to treat her as less than fully human, about the millions of Americans whose faith or lack of faith would be criminalized if Pastor Rick's vision became law. He thought about Jesus, who welcomed outsiders, rebuked religious leaders who used law to control, and insisted that faith must be free or it is not faith at all.

The fork in the road was getting clearer. Marcus could keep following his tribe's claim that "the Bible clearly says" whatever served their agenda, or he could follow Jesus, even when that meant rejecting the very people who had taught him to love Scripture in the first place.

# CHAPTER 5.

# WOMEN'S BODIES AND THE POLITICS OF CONTROL: WHEN "PRO-LIFE" POLICIES HARM THE VULNERABLE

**M**arcus's daughter Sarah was thirty-two weeks pregnant with her second child when the complications started, and suddenly every conversation he'd heard at church about "life beginning at conception" felt far more complicated than it had from the safety of a pew. The doctors used words like "preeclampsia" and "emergency delivery" and "we need to act fast," and Marcus found himself wondering, for the first time in his life, what would happen if Sarah lived in one of the states where his pastor had celebrated new abortion restrictions as a victory for God.

The question kept him awake that night in the hospital waiting room, and it wouldn't let go even after Sarah and the baby came through safely, because Marcus had spent years nodding along when Pastor Rick framed abortion as the defining moral issue of the age, the litmus test that separated faithful Christians from compromisers. He'd signed petitions, voted accordingly, and believed without question that stricter laws meant more protection for the unborn and a more godly nation. But watching his daughter's face flush as her blood pressure spiked, hearing the urgency in the doctor's voice, Marcus realized he'd never seriously considered what these laws would mean for women facing medical emergencies, women like Sarah, women he loved.

This chapter examines the gap between Christian nationalist "pro-life" rhetoric and the real-world consequences of policies that restrict abortion access, limit contraception, and chronically underfund maternal health care. Women experiencing miscarriages and ectopic pregnancies are being turned away from emergency rooms or forced to wait until they are critically ill and near death before doctors will intervene, because physicians fear prosecution under vague and punitive laws. Maternal mortality rates—already among the highest in the industrialized world—are climbing, and the burden falls heaviest on the women who can least afford it: poor women, Black women, and women in rural areas with limited access to care.

This chapter walks through the concrete fruit of these policies in women's lives, how restrictions on reproductive health care endanger mothers, worsen outcomes for infants, and create impossible choices for families already stretched thin. It then applies the Jesus Principle, testing whether abortion bans, contraception and in vitro fertilization (IVF) restrictions, and neglected maternal health care bear the fruit of the Spirit, protect the vulnerable, honor the Golden Rule, and align with medical reality and the way of Jesus.

By the end, Marcus will be forced to admit that the "pro-life" label he's worn for decades has too often been a cover for policies that control women more than they cherish life, and that following Jesus in this arena will require him to center the women whose voices have been drowned out by slogans and whose bodies have become battlegrounds in someone else's culture war. The question is no longer whether abortion is complicated; the question is whether Marcus is willing to let the lives of real women—including his own daughter—reshape what faithfulness looks like.

## The Fruit of Abortion Bans: Maternal Mortality, Medical Emergencies, and Real Women's Lives

Maternal deaths are rising fastest where bans are strictest. The data from states that enacted strict abortion bans after the Dobbs decision reveals a troubling pattern: maternal mortality rates have climbed sharply in banned states while declining in states that maintained abortion access.[47][49] Researchers forecast dozens of additional maternal deaths and thousands of severe complications in the most restrictive states.[46] Mothers in banned states faced nearly twice the risk of death during pregnancy, childbirth, or postpartum compared to those in states with legal abortion access, while supportive states saw maternal deaths decline.[47]

The burden lands hardest on Black and Latina women. In banned states, Black women faced maternal death rates several times higher than White women.[47] Among the eleven states with the highest maternal mortality rates between 2020 and 2022, eight now enforce total abortion bans.[52]

Delays in care are driving preventable emergencies. Beyond mortality statistics, abortion restrictions have driven increases in life-threatening complications that medical professionals describe as preventable. Texas saw a sharp spike in life threatening infections after its six-week ban, especially in pregnancies that were already doomed but could not be ended promptly.[48] Clinicians interviewed by researchers at the University of California, San Francisco, described being unable to offer the standard of care, forced to wait until women became critically ill or fetal cardiac activity ceased, even when the pregnancy was already nonviable and the mother's health was deteriorating.[48]

These delays produce precisely the outcomes that "pro-life" rhetoric claims to prevent. Over sixty percent of maternal deaths in the United States are considered preventable, with two-thirds occurring in the postpartum period, a window when policy barriers to timely care prove especially deadly.[51] Since Dobbs, banned states have seen tens of thousands of additional births and hundreds of preventable infant deaths, with the burden falling heaviest on Black, Hispanic, and other minority women and their children.[48][50]

When Marcus applies the Jesus Principle to these outcomes, the questions become unavoidable. Does a policy that doubles maternal mortality risk and drives preventable sepsis deaths bear the fruit of the Spirit? Does forcing women to carry nonviable pregnancies until they become critically ill protect the vulnerable, or does it sacrifice mothers—especially poor and Black mothers—on the altar of ideological purity? Would Marcus want his own daughter turned away from an emergency room during a miscarriage because doctors feared prosecution?

## Contraception, Maternal Health Care, and the Vulnerable Women Left Behind

While abortion bans dominate headlines, Christian nationalist agendas quietly target contraception access, leaving the most vulnerable women with fewer resources to prevent unintended pregnancies, manage chronic conditions, or survive childbirth.[53][54][55] These restrictions rest on the same premise as abortion bans, that life begins at conception and that any intervention preventing implantation is treated as abortion.[53][55][57]

At least nineteen states have enacted laws or constitutional amendments defining personhood at conception, creating legal uncertainty around contraceptive methods that may prevent a fertilized egg from implanting in the uterine wall, including IUDs and emergency contraception.[53] Pharmacists in multiple states have refused to fill prescriptions for emergency contraception, citing religious objections, while legislative proposals seek to exclude contraception from insurance coverage mandates. These barriers fall hardest on low-income women who rely on employer-sponsored insurance or publicly funded clinics for affordable contraception, forcing many to forgo the most effective methods or go without entirely.[55][56]

The consequences extend beyond individual choice. Access to contraception is a cornerstone of maternal health strategy, allowing women to space pregnancies, manage chronic conditions like diabetes or hypertension that complicate pregnancy, and reduce the risk of maternal mortality. Research consistently shows that unintended pregnancies carry higher risks of poor prenatal care, preterm birth, and maternal complications. When contraception becomes harder to obtain, unintended pregnancy rates rise, and the women least equipped to navigate high-risk pregnancies—those without reliable transportation, health insurance, or proximity to specialized care—bear the greatest burden.[55][56]

There is a simple way to test whether the goal is truly to reduce abortions or to control women's bodies: look at whether leaders embrace the strategies that actually lower abortion rates. States and countries that combine comprehensive, science-based sex education with easy access to effective contraception—especially long-acting reversible methods—see significant drops in unintended pregnancy and abortion, particularly among teens and young adults. Colorado's statewide initiative to provide no-cost IUDs and implants to low-income women, for example, dramatically reduced teen births and abortions, all without criminalizing women or threatening doctors.

If "prolife" were primarily about preventing abortions, these proven approaches would be at the center of every Christian nationalist platform and pulpit. Instead, many of the same lawmakers who champion bans on abortion also oppose comprehensive sex education, fight public funding for contraception, and support policies that make it harder—not easier—for sexually active teens and low-income women to access birth control. When the tools that most effectively reduce abortions are rejected while criminal penalties and control over women's sexuality are expanded, the fruit reveals the true priorities.

The same ideology that targets abortion and contraception is hollowing out basic care. Maternal health care infrastructure in the United States is already fragile, particularly in rural areas and states with restrictive abortion laws. Large swaths of the country, especially rural areas, now lack basic maternity services, forcing women to travel long distances for prenatal and emergency care. The post-*Dobbs* environment has accelerated clinic closures and physician departures in ban states, as providers fear prosecution and malpractice liability under vague exceptions for maternal health emergencies.[53][54] Women in these regions must travel hours for prenatal care, increasing the likelihood of missed appointments, undiagnosed complications, and delayed intervention when emergencies arise.

Christian nationalist policy proposals, including those outlined in Project 2025, advocate eliminating federal funding for family planning programs, and rolling back Medicaid expansion that has extended prenatal and postpartum coverage to low-income mothers.[53][54] These measures strip away the safety net that keeps maternal mortality from climbing even higher, particularly for Black and Indigenous women who already face maternal death rates two to three times higher than White women due to systemic inequities in care quality and access.[55][56]

When Marcus applies the Jesus Principle to these policies, the questions cut through the rhetoric. Does restricting contraception and defunding maternal health programs bear the fruit of the Spirit when it increases unintended pregnancies, maternal deaths, and infant mortality? Would Marcus want his own daughter denied birth control by her employer, forced to drive three hours for prenatal care, or left without postpartum Medicaid coverage? And is it true that these policies protect life, when the evidence shows they endanger the women whose lives should matter just as much as the pregnancies they carry?[53][54]

## The Jesus Principle Test:
## Would You Want This for Your Daughter?

Marcus had spent years defending abortion restrictions as biblical obedience, but now he found himself asking a question he'd never allowed before: What if the woman facing these laws were Sarah? What if it were his granddaughter twenty years from now? The Golden Rule—*do to others as you would have them do to you*—had always seemed simple in Sunday school but applying it to the policies he'd championed felt like standing on shifting ground.

The Jesus Principle's third question cuts through abstract ideology by forcing a concrete, personal test: *Would I want this done to me or to those I love?* When applied to Christian nationalist restrictions on women's reproductive health care, the question becomes unavoidable: Would you want these outcomes for your own daughter?

The answer for most parents is immediate and visceral: No. No parent wants their daughter turned away from an emergency room during a miscarriage because doctors fear prosecution. No father wants his pregnant daughter's life endangered by laws that delay standard medical care until she is critically ill. No mother wants her child denied contraception by an employer's religious objection, left without postpartum Medicaid coverage, or forced to carry a pregnancy resulting from rape because the state has decided her body is not her own.

Yet these are precisely the outcomes that abortion bans and related restrictions produce in the lives of other people's daughters.[29] [30] [32] [34] Research from states with the strictest bans shows maternal mortality climbing sharply, with Black women facing death rates more than three times higher than White women. Women experiencing ectopic pregnancies and inevitable miscarriages report being sent home from hospitals because physicians cannot risk prosecution under vague "life of the mother" exceptions.

The Golden Rule test exposes the moral failure at the heart of Christian nationalist "pro-life" politics: these policies demand sacrifices from vulnerable women that their architects and defenders would never accept for their own families. Legislators who vote for total abortion bans ensure their own daughters have resources to travel for care if needed. Pastors who preach against contraception access often belong to communities where private insurance and family wealth provide a safety net unavailable to the working poor. The burden of forced pregnancy, delayed emergency care, and inadequate maternal health services falls overwhelmingly on women who lack the money, mobility, and political power to escape it.

When Marcus imagines Sarah facing the consequences of the laws he supported—denied timely care during a complication, prosecuted for a miscarriage, or forced to continue a pregnancy that endangers her life—the abstractions collapse. The slogans about "protecting the unborn" and "biblical values" cannot survive the simple question Jesus himself commanded his followers to ask: *How would I want to be treated?*

This is not a call to abandon concern for prenatal life or to dismiss the moral weight of abortion. For many Christians, unborn children are themselves among the vulnerable whom God cares about, and that conviction should not be mocked or ignored. The Jesus Principle does not ask us to stop valuing prenatal life; it asks whether the policies we support genuinely protect all the vulnerable, or whether they protect some at the expense of others—especially the women whose lives and bodies are most at risk. It is a call to recognize that any ethic claiming to follow Jesus must pass the test Jesus gave: love of neighbor measured by love of self, protection of the vulnerable measured by what we would demand for our own children, and policies evaluated not by their slogans but by their fruit in real women's lives.

The Jesus Principle test reveals that Christian nationalist restrictions on women's bodies fail precisely where Jesus' teaching is clearest. They do not protect the vulnerable but instead endanger them, even when they claim to defend another vulnerable life in the womb. They collapse under the Golden Rule the moment we imagine our own loved ones subject to their power. And they rest on selective truths and medical falsehoods that obscure the harm they cause. For Marcus, the question is no longer whether these policies are complicated; the question is whether he can call them Christian when he would never want them for Sarah.

Marcus sat in the hospital cafeteria long after Sarah and the baby had been moved to recovery, staring at his cold coffee and replaying the last seventy-two hours in his mind. He kept thinking about the moment when the doctor had said, "We need to act fast," and how grateful he'd been that Sarah lived in a state where physicians could still make medical decisions without consulting lawyers first. And he realized, with a clarity that felt both liberating and terrifying, that he could no longer call those bans "pro-life" when the data showed they were ending and endangering lives instead.

The Jesus Principle exposes the gap between slogans and fruit with uncomfortable precision. Policies that raise maternal mortality and drive preventable sepsis deaths do not bear the fruit of the Spirit in women's lives. Forcing mothers to carry nonviable pregnancies until they become critically ill does not protect the vulnerable but sacrifices them—especially poor women and women of color—on the altar of ideological purity.

What this chapter has argued is that any ethic claiming to follow Jesus must pass the test Jesus gave: love of neighbor measured by love of self, protection of the vulnerable measured by what we would demand for our own children, and policies evaluated not by their rhetoric but by their fruit in real lives.

For Marcus, the turning point came when he stopped evaluating these policies from the safety of abstract principle and started asking what they would mean for Sarah, for his granddaughters, and for the women in his church whose names he knew. The question Jesus commanded his followers to ask—*How would I want to be treated?*—proved more powerful than any slogan about protecting the unborn, because it forced him to see the women being harmed in the name of his faith.

Marcus could see now that if the real goal had been fewer abortions, leaders would have championed the prevention strategies that work instead of rejecting them. Christian nationalist restrictions on women's bodies are, at best, hard to reconcile with the way Jesus treated women; they look far more like the politics of control than the compassion of Christ. Marcus could no longer call that faithfulness, and he was realizing that following Jesus would require him to say so.

# CHAPTER 6.

# RACE, CHOSENNESS, AND THE MYTH OF THE "REAL AMERICAN"

Marcus had never thought of himself as racist—he had Black colleagues at work, his church's worship team was diverse, and he'd voted for policies he believed would help everyone—but the conversation at his men's Bible study that morning had left him unsettled in a way he couldn't quite name. When someone mentioned the new voter ID requirements and another man said, "Well, real Americans shouldn't have a problem showing ID," Marcus noticed how everyone nodded, and he found himself wondering who, exactly, didn't count as "real."

The question had been nagging at him for weeks now, ever since he'd started paying closer attention to the language swirling through his church, his news feeds, and the political rallies his pastor had been promoting from the pulpit. There was always talk of "taking our country back" and "restoring America's Christian heritage," but Marcus was beginning to notice a pattern in who was imagined as part of that restoration and who was framed as a threat to it. The heroes in these stories were almost always white, almost always native-born, almost always Christian in a very specific cultural sense. The villains—the people depicted as invaders, fraudsters, criminals, and dangers to the social order—were almost never white.

This chapter pulls back the curtain on one of Christian nationalism's most toxic features: its fusion of national chosenness with assumptions about race, belonging, and who counts as a legitimate American. Beneath the rhetoric of "biblical values" and "God's plan for America" lies a story in which the nation is imagined as specially elected by God, and White Christians are cast as its rightful heirs and protectors. This is not mere patriotism or even garden-variety nationalism; it is a racialized vision of divine favor that has been used for centuries to justify exclusion, exploitation, and violence against Black, Indigenous, Latino, Asian, and immigrant communities.

The chapter traces how this "chosenness" narrative shows up in concrete policy debates today, not as overt racial slurs, which have largely been driven underground, but as coded appeals to "law and order," "election integrity," "border security," and "parental rights" in education. Research consistently shows that the stronger someone's Christian nationalist convictions, the more likely they are to support restrictive voting laws, harsh immigration enforcement, punitive criminal justice policies, and school curricula that avoid honest reckoning with racism. These positions are rarely defended in explicitly racial terms anymore, but their effects are anything but race-neutral: they systematically disadvantage communities of color while protecting the comfort, power, and political influence of White Americans.

Marcus's journey in this chapter is one of painful recognition. As he listens more carefully to the stories his church tells about America, he begins to see who is always centered as the protagonist and who is always cast as the problem. He notices that when his pastor talks about "our heritage" and "our freedoms," the "our" never seems to include his Black coworker whose grandfather was denied the vote, or the Latino families at his daughter's school who live in fear of immigration raids, or the Indigenous activists he saw dismissed as "anti-American" for protesting a pipeline on their own land.

By the end of the chapter, Marcus will be forced to ask whether the "real American" he has been taught to defend is a category that was ever meant to include everyone, or whether it has always been a way of saying "White" and "Christian" without having to say it out loud.

And he will have to run the policies that flow from this vision—policies on voting, immigration, policing, and education—through the four questions of the Jesus Principle, asking what kind of fruit they bear in the lives of his Black and brown neighbors, whether they protect or harm the vulnerable, and whether he would want to live under them if his own family were on the receiving end.

## The Chosenness Story:
## White Christian America as God's Elect Nation

The story that White Christian America has told itself for centuries is a story of divine election. It borrows the language and imagery of ancient Israel—God's chosen people, set apart for a sacred purpose, called to be a light to the nations—and maps it directly onto the United States, with one crucial addition: the assumption that White Christians are the rightful heirs and guardians of that chosenness.[58][59] This is not a fringe idea confined to extremist groups; it is woven deeply into the fabric of American civil religion, shaping how millions of Christians understand their nation's identity, their own place in it, and the threats they believe endanger both.

Historians trace this "chosenness narrative" to the earliest days of European colonization.[59] By around 1690, nearly a century before the United States existed as a nation, the story was already fully formed: America was imagined as a new Israel, a covenant land where God's elect people would build a society ordered by Protestant Christian principles and spread the gospel to a world mired in darkness.[58][59] This vision integrated three biblical motifs—the Chosen People story, the End Times story, and what scholars call the Racial Curse story—into a single, powerful myth that cast White Protestant settlers as God's agents and Native peoples, enslaved Africans, and later waves of Catholic and non-Christian immigrants as obstacles, threats, or objects of divine judgment.[58]

By the late nineteenth century, this theology had hardened into explicit racial supremacy. Josiah Strong's widely read book *Our Country*, published in 1885, declared the United States "God's right arm in his battle with the world's ignorance and oppression and sin" and identified Anglo-Saxon Protestants as "the elect nation . . . the chosen people" destined to lead Christianity's final global conflicts.[60] Strong was not an outlier; he was articulating what much of White Protestant America already believed.[60] The nation's prosperity, its territorial expansion, its growing power on the world stage—all were read as evidence of divine favor, proof that God had specially chosen this people for this land.

This narrative did not fade with the end of the frontier or the civil rights movement. It adapted. Today's Christian nationalism rarely uses the overt racial language of Josiah Strong, but the underlying logic remains: America is a White Christian nation, and its power and prosperity depend on maintaining the dominance of White Christians over racial, religious, and national "others."[58][59] Polling data reveals the persistence of this worldview. Among Americans who perceive significant discrimination against White people, 59 percent favor declaring the United States officially a Christian nation, a rate far higher than among those who do not share that perception of White grievance.[62] The chosenness story and White racial anxiety are deeply intertwined.

Scholars who study the spatial practices of White evangelicalism have documented how this narrative is reinforced in everyday religious life.[61] Tours of Washington, D.C., marketed to conservative Christian groups, for example, emphasize the presence of White Christians in American history while systematically excluding the contributions and experiences of Black, Indigenous, Latino, Asian, and non-Christian communities.[61] Visitors are taught to see minor religious symbols on monuments as "evidence" of a Christian founding, while the histories of slavery, Native dispossession, and religious pluralism are minimized or erased.[61] The result is a curated memory that centers whiteness and Christianity as the nation's true heritage and casts everyone else as footnotes or threats.

This is the deep story beneath Christian nationalist politics: not simply that America should honor God, but that White Christians are God's elect stewards of the nation, and any loss of White Christian cultural or political dominance represents a betrayal of divine purpose.[58][59] It is a story that has justified centuries of exclusion and violence, and it continues to shape policy debates today in ways that demand scrutiny through the lens of Jesus' teaching.

## Policy and Practice: How "Real American" Rhetoric Shapes Voting, Immigration, and Policing

The "chosenness" narrative does not remain abstract theology. It translates directly into concrete policy preferences that systematically advantage White Americans while disadvantaging communities of color, and research consistently shows that Christian nationalism strongly predicts support for restrictive voting laws, harsh immigration enforcement, and punitive criminal justice policies.[62][63]

Sociologists Andrew Whitehead and Samuel Perry have documented these patterns across multiple studies.[65] Their work shows that Christian nationalism is among the strongest predictors of opposition to policies that would expand access to the ballot, with adherents significantly more likely to support strict voter identification requirements, purges of voter rolls, and reductions in early voting periods.[62][65][66] These measures are typically justified in race-neutral language about "election integrity" and ensuring that only "real Americans" vote, but their effects are anything but neutral. Empirical analyses of voter ID laws and registration restrictions show that they disproportionately reduce turnout among Black, Latino, and low-income voters, the very communities that Christian nationalist rhetoric often codes as less authentically American.[62][63]

The same pattern appears in immigration policy. Christian nationalism strongly predicts support for border walls, mass deportation, family separation, and asylum restrictions, with adherents more likely to view immigrants—especially those from Latin America, Muslim-majority countries, or other non-Christian regions—as cultural and spiritual threats rather than neighbors in need.[62][63][64] This xenophobia is not incidental to the ideology but flows directly from its fusion of national identity with a particular religious and racial vision.[62][63] When the nation is imagined as a covenant land entrusted to White Christians, welcoming the stranger becomes a betrayal of divine purpose rather than an act of obedience to Jesus' command.[62][63]

Policing and criminal justice reveal the same logic. Research links Christian nationalism with strong support for law-and-order politics, including tolerance for aggressive policing in communities of color, opposition to police accountability measures, and hostility toward movements like Black Lives Matter.[62][63] Because the "real American" is presumed to be law-abiding, Christian, and White, crime and social disorder are racialized and externalized, and attributed to urban, Black, immigrant, or secular populations who fall outside the idealized national body.[62][63] Police are symbolically aligned with the defense of Christian America, and calls for reform or accountability are interpreted as attacks on the guardians of the moral order rather than as efforts to ensure equal justice.[62][63]

Educational policy completes the picture. Christian nationalists are significantly more likely to oppose curricula that teach honestly about slavery, segregation, and ongoing racial inequality, framing such instruction as "divisive" or "anti-American."[62][63] This resistance protects the chosenness narrative by preventing students from encountering evidence that the nation's history and present are shaped by exclusion and exploitation rather than divine favor.[62][63] The effect is to preserve White comfort and cultural dominance while denying communities of color the recognition and repair that truth-telling might require.[62][63]

Marcus had never connected these dots before. He had supported voter ID laws because they seemed like common sense, backed immigration restrictions because he believed in the rule of law, and trusted that police were simply doing a hard job in dangerous neighborhoods. But as he began to notice the pattern—who these policies protected and who they punished, who was imagined as the threat and who as the victim—he could no longer ignore the question of whose America was being defended and at whose expense.[62][63] The "real American" his church celebrated looked like him, sounded like him, and voted like him, and everyone else was expected to accept a permanently subordinate place or be cast as the enemy within.[62][63]

# The Jesus Principle Test:
## Fruit, Vulnerability, and the Golden Rule Across Racial Lines

Marcus had spent the last hour reading through his church's prayer requests and political action alerts side by side, and the pattern was impossible to miss: every policy his congregation celebrated as "biblical" seemed to land hardest on his Black and Latino neighbors, while every threat they prayed against seemed to involve people who didn't look like the folks in his pews. He decided it was time to run these positions through the four questions he'd been learning, starting with the simplest one: What fruit do these policies actually bear in the lives of people on the other side of the racial line?

When Christian nationalist positions on voting, immigration, policing, and education are evaluated through the Jesus Principle's four questions, a consistent pattern emerges: they fail to produce the fruit of the Spirit in communities of color, they harm rather than protect vulnerable neighbors, they collapse under the Golden Rule when one imagines being on the receiving end, and they often rest on misleading or selective claims about history and social reality.[8][9][11]

**Does it bear good fruit?** Research on voter identification laws and registration restrictions shows that these measures, typically justified as protecting "election integrity," disproportionately reduce turnout among Black, Latino, and low-income voters without meaningfully preventing fraud. The fruit in affected communities is not greater confidence in democracy but increased barriers to participation, longer wait times at polling places in minority neighborhoods, and the message that some citizens' votes are presumed illegitimate until proven otherwise.[9] Immigration enforcement policies supported by Christian nationalists—including mass deportation, family separation, and asylum restrictions—produce fruit of fear and trauma in immigrant communities, with children experiencing toxic stress, families torn apart, and entire neighborhoods living under the threat of raids.[9] Aggressive policing practices and opposition to accountability measures yield fruit of mistrust, over-incarceration of Black and brown men, and cycles of violence rather than the safety and flourishing that love, peace, and gentleness would produce.[9]

**Does it care for the vulnerable?** Looking at these policies through the second question—how they treat those with the least power—Marcus saw another pattern emerge. Voter ID laws and registration purges fall hardest on elderly Black voters, low-income workers with inflexible jobs, and citizens without easy access to transportation or underlying documents. Immigration crackdowns expose mixed-status families, refugees, and longtime residents to constant fear and the risk of family separation. Aggressive policing and harsh sentencing concentrate harm in poor Black and Latino neighborhoods, where residents already face fewer economic opportunities and less access to quality schools and health care. The people with the least margin for error carry the heaviest burden of these policies, while those with the most resources remain largely insulated.

**Would I want this done to me or those I love?** The Golden Rule becomes especially sharp when applied across racial lines.[8][9][11] Marcus began asking himself: Would I want my own family subjected to the voter ID requirements that force elderly Black citizens to travel hours for documents they've never needed before? Would I want my children growing up in neighborhoods where immigration enforcement means any interaction with authorities could result in a parent's deportation? Would I want my son treated the way young Black men are treated in traffic stops, or sentenced the way they are sentenced for the same offenses White defendants commit? When he imagined his own loved ones on the receiving end of these policies, the answers were immediate and uncomfortable. He would not want this for his family, and the realization forced him to confront whether he could in good conscience support policies for others that he would never accept for himself.[8][9][11]

**Is it true?** Christian nationalist rhetoric about voting fraud, immigrant crime, and urban disorder relies on selective facts and racialized fears rather than comprehensive evidence.[9] Large-scale studies of voter fraud find it exceedingly rare, undermining claims that strict ID laws are necessary to protect elections. Data on immigration and crime show that immigrants, including undocumented immigrants, commit crimes at lower rates than native-born citizens, contradicting the "invasion" narrative.[9] Yet these facts are routinely ignored in favor of anecdotes and fear-based appeals that code Black and brown communities as threats to the social order.[9]

Marcus realized that the "real American" story his church had been telling was never race-neutral. It had always centered White Christians as the protagonists and cast communities of color as problems to be managed, threats to be contained, or outsiders whose full participation must be limited.[89] Running these positions through the Jesus Principle revealed that they were not neutral at all but consistently harmed Black and brown communities while claiming God's blessing.

Marcus closed his notebook and sat in silence, the weight of the last few weeks pressing down on him in a way that felt both unbearable and strangely clarifying. He had spent his entire adult life believing that loving his country and following Jesus were essentially the same thing, that the "real America" his church celebrated was simply the nation as God intended it to be. But now, after tracing the threads of the chosenness narrative through voting restrictions, immigration raids, policing practices, and school board battles, he could no longer ignore the pattern. The "real American" story had always been a story about who belonged and who didn't, and the dividing line had never been drawn by Jesus.

The research Marcus had encountered over the past month painted a picture he could no longer unsee. Christian nationalism was not a race-neutral theology that happened to have disparate effects; it was a racialized ideology from its origins, fusing divine election with White cultural dominance and coding threats to that dominance as threats to God's plan.

When Marcus ran these issues through the four questions of the Jesus Principle, the verdict was unambiguous. Instead of the fruit of the Spirit in the lives of his Black and brown neighbors, they produced fear, exclusion, disenfranchisement, and harm. They did not protect the vulnerable; they targeted them, stripping away voting access, family stability, physical safety, and educational honesty in the name of preserving a social order that had never included them as equals. They collapsed under the Golden Rule the moment Marcus imagined his own family subjected to the same treatment, his own children denied the vote, his own grandchildren living in fear of deportation, his own son policed and sentenced the way young Black men are policed and sentenced. And they rested on selective facts and racialized myths rather than the full truth about American history, immigrant contributions, or the actual sources of social disorder.

Most painfully, Marcus realized that the Jesus he claimed to follow had spent his entire ministry dismantling precisely this kind of insider-outsider logic. Jesus had centered Samaritans, tax collectors, women, lepers, and foreigners—the people his own religious community treated as threats and outsiders—and he had reserved his harshest words for those who used religious authority to justify exclusion and dominance. The "chosenness" that mattered to Jesus was never about ethnicity, nationality, or cultural power; it was about being chosen to serve, to welcome, to lay down privilege rather than weaponize it. A faith that protected the comfort of the powerful while sacrificing the dignity and safety of the marginalized was not the faith Jesus taught, no matter how many Bible verses defended it.

Marcus knew that what came next would not be easy. Naming the racialized logic beneath Christian nationalism meant confronting his own complicity, his own comfort, and his own community's investment in a story that had always placed people who looked like him at the center. But he also knew that he could not follow Jesus and continue to support policies that failed every test Jesus had given. The fork in the road was real, and the choice was his to make.

# CHAPTER 7.

# PROTECTING THE FAMILY OR TARGETING OUR KIDS? FAITH AND FREEDOM IN THE LIVES OF LGBTQ+ YOUTH

T he photo on Marcus's phone showed his grandson Ethan at his eighth birthday party, grinning gap-toothed over a superhero cake, and Marcus found himself staring at it longer than usual after the school board meeting he'd just attended. The meeting had been packed with parents demanding the removal of library books that mentioned LGBTQ+ families, and someone from his church had testified that "these books are grooming our children," but all Marcus could think about now was a simple question: What if one day Ethan needed one of those books? What if the child who felt alone, confused, and afraid was his own grandchild, and the adults who claimed to be protecting him had stripped away every resource that might have helped him feel less alone and isolated?

The question unsettled Marcus in a way he hadn't expected. For years he had heard "family values" framed as a clear line in the sand— traditional marriage, biblical gender roles, protecting children from "the agenda"—and he had nodded along, confident that standing firm on these issues was simply what faithfulness required. But tonight, holding Ethan's picture in his hand, Marcus realized he had never seriously asked what these policies actually did to real children and real families, especially those who didn't fit the mold his church had taught him to defend.

This chapter examines how Christian nationalist rhetoric around "protecting the family" and "parental rights" often produces environments of exclusion, shame, and serious harm for LGBTQ+ youth and their families. Framed as safeguarding children from danger, these campaigns frequently strip away the very support systems that vulnerable young people need most: affirming adults, accurate information, mental health resources, and legal protections against discrimination. The result is not stronger families but fractured ones, not safer children but more isolated and at-risk adolescents.

The chapter walks through the landscape of policies and cultural battles waged in the name of family values—book bans, curriculum restrictions, rollbacks of antibullying protections, and attacks on gender-affirming care—and then applies the Jesus Principle to ask what kind of fruit they bear in the lives of LGBTQ+ youth.

The Golden Rule question becomes especially piercing here: Would Marcus want these policies applied to his own grandchild? Would he want Ethan—or any child he loves—subjected to laws and church cultures that treat difference as danger, that offer shame instead of support, and that prioritize ideological purity over the well-being of vulnerable kids? When Marcus imagines his own family on the receiving end of these "protective" measures, the gap between Christian nationalist family values and the way of Jesus becomes impossible to ignore.

By the chapter's end, Marcus must wrestle with whether his commitment to defending "biblical family values" would survive if someone he loves came out. Readers are invited to ask the same question and to consider what it would mean to build families and communities that truly protect all children—especially those most at risk—by reflecting Jesus' fierce defense of the vulnerable and his radical welcome of those the religious establishment cast aside.

# The "Family Values" Frame: Who Counts as Family Worth Protecting?

Christian nationalist rhetoric consistently invokes "family values" as a rallying cry, but the families deemed worthy of protection under this banner are narrowly defined and strictly policed. The frame privileges a specific model: a hierarchical nuclear unit consisting of a married heterosexual couple—with the husband as head of household—and their biological or adopted children, all adhering to conservative gender roles and Protestant Christian norms.[12 67 68] This vision is presented not merely as one legitimate family structure among many but as the divinely ordained foundation of national strength and moral order.[12 67]

Project 2025's *Mandate for Leadership* makes this explicit, asserting that "families comprised of a married mother, father, and their children are the foundation of a well-ordered nation and healthy society."[12] The document goes on to advocate policies that promote this nuclear model while critiquing single-parent households and non-traditional family structures as sources of societal decay.[12] The implication is clear: families that do not conform to this template are not simply different but deficient, even dangerous.

This narrow definition enforces a social hierarchy that places certain families—White, cisgender, heterosexual, Protestant—at the center of American identity while relegating others to the margins or casting them as threats.[12 68 70] LGBTQ+ families, single parent households, and families led by non-Christians, and any structure that deviates from the prescribed gender roles are vilified as immoral and destabilizing.[67 68 70] Research consistently links Christian nationalism to opposition against LGBTQ+ rights, support for traditional gender hierarchies, and resistance to policies that recognize diverse family forms as equally legitimate.[70]

The ideology frames conformity to this family model as essential for national survival, often tying it to fears of moral decline and social disorder.[12 67] Legislative efforts reflect this priority: laws mandating displays of the Ten Commandments in public schools are justified as necessary to instill respect for authority and traditional morality, implicitly excluding families rooted in other faith traditions or secular values.[68] Campaigns to remove library books featuring LGBTQ+ characters or diverse family structures are framed as protecting children, yet they function to erase the existence of families that fall outside the approved mold.

Christian nationalism treats the family as the primary site for instilling sectarian Protestant values—strict gender roles, obedience to male authority, and heterosexual norms. Children raised in families that do not conform are seen as inadequately socialized, vulnerable to "gender ideology" or "the LGBTQ+ agenda," and in need of correction by the state or church.[68] This extends to support for policies that allow parents to restrict school curricula that acknowledge diverse families, and roll back anti-discrimination protections, all in the name of parental rights and religious freedom.

The result is a framework that protects some families by targeting others. Families that align with Christian nationalist ideals receive legal privileges, cultural affirmation, and institutional support. Families that do not—especially those with LGBTQ+ members, single parents, or non-Christian identities—face legal barriers, social stigma, and the withdrawal of resources designed to support vulnerable children and parents.[12 67 68] The "family values" frame thus functions not as a universal commitment to family well-being but as a tool for enforcing conformity and maintaining hierarchies of power.

When Marcus stared at the photo of his grandson and asked what would happen if Ethan needed the very resources his church was working to remove, he was beginning to see through the frame. The question of who counts as family worth protecting is not answered by appeals to biblical tradition or national heritage but by examining whose children are centered in policy and whose are sacrificed, whose parents are honored and whose are shamed, and whether the fruit of these "family values" campaigns is greater flourishing or greater harm for the most vulnerable among us.

## The Real Fruit in Young Lives:
## Mental Health, Suicide Risk, and Belonging

The rhetoric of protecting children sounds noble, but the actual outcomes in the lives of LGBTQ+ youth tell a starkly different story. When policies and church cultures frame LGBTQ+ identities as threats to be eliminated rather than realities to be acknowledged with compassion, the fruit borne in young lives is measurably harmful: elevated rates of depression, anxiety, self-harm, and suicidal ideation that far exceed those of their peers.

Research from The Trevor Project's 2020 national survey of 40,000 LGBTQ+ youth found that 40 percent seriously contemplated suicide in the past year, with rates exceeding 50 percent among transgender and nonbinary youth.[71] Suicide ranks as the second-leading cause of death for individuals aged ten to twenty-four, and nearly half of surveyed youth reported seeking but being unable to obtain psychological or emotional counseling.[71] The COVID-19 pandemic intensified isolation, with 40 percent unable to access care due to parental concerns.[71] These are not abstract statistics but the lived reality of children sitting in classrooms, youth groups, and family dinner tables across the country.

The gap between these outcomes and Christian nationalist claims of protecting children is impossible to ignore. Instead, they undermine the very supports that research shows are essential for reducing risk and fostering resilience in vulnerable adolescents.

The protective power of acceptance is equally well documented. Transgender and nonbinary youth whose chosen pronouns are respected by all or most people in their lives attempt suicide at half the rate of those whose pronouns are not respected.[71] Family support dramatically reduces mental health disparities, while rejection—often rooted in theological frameworks that label LGBTQ+ identities as inherently sinful or disordered—intensifies isolation and distress.[71] The American Psychiatric Association has stated clearly that access to gender-affirming care in adolescence decreases suicide risk, yet

Christian nationalist agendas seek to criminalize such care and punish parents who provide it.[75]

Religious environments themselves can become sites of profound harm when they communicate that LGBTQ+ youth are unwelcome or fundamentally broken. Nearly two-thirds of LGBTQ+ adults raised Christian no longer identify as such, and those who leave report higher rates of childhood bullying and internalized shame.[72] National survey data links stronger Christian nationalist beliefs to greater religious and spiritual struggles, emotional distress, depression, and anxiety.[73] [76] When faith communities frame LGBTQ+ identities as threats to children and Christian culture—as seen in over 160 bills targeting LGBTQ+ youth introduced in early 2023 alone—they create environments where vulnerable young people learn that their churches, schools, and families view them not as beloved children but as problems to be solved or dangers to be contained.[74]

The words of faith leaders underscore the urgency. Jun Young, founder of Beloved Arise, has said, "LGBTQ+ kids are in your care and some of them are hanging on by a thread. We have to take immediate steps to ensure our environments are safe for all kids."[71] Austen Hartke, author of *Transforming: The Bible and the Lives of Transgender Christians*, notes that when attempted suicide rates for transgender youth are three times those of straight cisgender youth, "our churches should be actively creating plans to support our young people . . . So why not make church one of those places?"[71]

The fruit of Christian nationalist "family values" campaigns in the lives of LGBTQ+ youth is not protection but harm, not flourishing but isolation, not life but measurably increased risk of death. When Marcus imagined his own grandson needing the resources his church was working to remove, he was beginning to see what the data confirm: policies built on exclusion and shame do not protect children—they endanger the most vulnerable among them.

# The Jesus Principle Test:
## Would You Want This for Your Own Child?

The most piercing question in the Jesus Principle is also the simplest: Would you want this for your own child? This is the Golden Rule made personal and immediate, stripping away abstract theology and political talking points to expose what policies and church cultures actually demand of real families. When Marcus imagined his grandson Ethan on the receiving end of the laws and rhetoric his church had celebrated, the entire framework shifted from defending principles to protecting a child he loved.

The Golden Rule—"Do to others as you would have them do to you"—appears in every major religious tradition, but Jesus places it at the center of his teaching, calling it the summary of the Law and the Prophets. Applied to LGBTQ+ youth, the question becomes unavoidable: If your child came out as gay, transgender, or nonbinary, would you want them subjected to the policies Christian nationalism promotes in the name of protecting families?[29][30][31][32][34][77]

Would Marcus want Ethan's school library purged of every book that might help him understand himself or feel less alone? Would he want his grandson's teachers legally barred from acknowledging that families like his exist, forced to pretend that difference is too dangerous even to name? Would he want Ethan denied access to counseling that affirms his worth and helps him navigate a world that tells him he is broken? Would he want the state to criminalize parents who seek medical care their doctors recommend, threatening them with prosecution for supporting their own child?

The answer for most parents, when the child in question is their own, is immediate and visceral: No! Yet these are precisely the measures that Christian nationalist agendas advance under the banner of parental rights and religious freedom.[29][30][31][32][34][77] Project 2025's policy blueprint calls for eliminating federal protections against discrimination based on sexual orientation and gender identity, removing transgender students from Title IX coverage, and restricting access to gender-affirming care. State legislatures have introduced hundreds of bills targeting LGBTQ+ youth in schools, health care, and public accommodations, often with explicit support from Christian nationalist organizations that frame these efforts as defending children and families.[29] [30] [31] [32] [34] [77]

The gap between what parents would tolerate for their own children and what they support in the abstract reveals the failure of these policies under the Golden Rule. Research shows that family rejection dramatically increases suicide risk for LGBTQ+ youth, while acceptance and support cut that risk by more than half. When parents imagine their own child facing rejection, isolation, and the message that who they are is too shameful to acknowledge, most recognize instinctively that such treatment bears none of the fruit of the Spirit—not love, not kindness, not gentleness, not self-control—but instead produces fear, shame, and measurable harm.

Jesus' own treatment of children offers a stark contrast to Christian nationalist family politics. He welcomed those the religious establishment cast out, touched the untouchable, and insisted that the measure of faithfulness was not ideological purity but how one treated the least of these.

When Marcus held the photo of his grandson and asked what he would want for Ethan if Ethan were the one who needed help, the Jesus Principle cut through every layer of political rhetoric and theological abstraction. The test is not whether a policy can be defended with selective Bible verses or framed in the language of protection. The test is whether it reflects the kind of love, mercy, and fierce defense of vulnerable children that marked Jesus' own ministry, and whether those who promote it would accept the same treatment for the children they love most. Marcus sat in his truck long after the school board meeting ended, the photo of Ethan still glowing on his phone's screen. For years he had believed that defending "family values" meant drawing clear lines, standing firm on biblical truth, and protecting children from dangerous ideas. Tonight, he realized he had never asked the most important question: protecting them from what, and at what cost to the children who needed protection most?

The chapter has traced how Christian nationalist rhetoric around family and children consistently produces outcomes that contradict its stated goals. These campaigns strip away resources, affirming relationships, and accurate information that research shows are essential for reducing suicide risk and fostering resilience in LGBTQ+ adolescents.

The Jesus Principle exposes the gap between Christian nationalist family politics and the way of Jesus across all four questions. These policies do not bear the fruit of the Spirit in young lives; they produce measurably higher rates of depression, anxiety, self-harm, and suicidal ideation. They do not protect the vulnerable but instead harm the children most at risk, isolating them from support systems and communicating that their identities are too shameful to acknowledge. They fail the Golden Rule catastrophically: few parents would accept for their own children the exclusion, shame, and denial of care that these laws impose on other families. And they rest on claims about protecting children that are contradicted by the evidence of what actually happens when LGBTQ+ youth are rejected rather than affirmed.

Jesus placed children at the center of the kingdom, warned that harming them merited the severest judgment, and reserved his sharpest words for religious leaders who laid heavy burdens on the vulnerable while refusing to lift a finger to help. He welcomed those the religious establishment cast out and insisted that the measure of faithfulness was how one treated the least of these. Christian nationalism's approach to LGBTQ+ youth and non-conforming families inverts this priority, sacrificing vulnerable children to preserve ideological purity and using state power to enforce one narrow vision of family life on everyone.

Marcus could no longer pretend that defending family values and following Jesus were the same thing. One path led to policies that increased suffering for the most at-risk children in the name of protection. The other led to the kind of radical welcome and costly love that Jesus modeled, even—especially—for those the religious gatekeepers wanted to exclude. The question was no longer whether LGBTQ+ youth and their families fit his theology. The question was whether his theology produced the kind of fruit Jesus said would mark his followers, and whether he was willing to choose Jesus over tribe when the two pointed in opposite directions.

# CHAPTER 8.

# LAW, ORDER, AND LOVING OUR ENEMIES: THE SERMON ON THE MOUNT MEETS THE POLITICS OF FEAR

Marcus had Matthew 5 open on his kitchen table—"Blessed are the peacemakers," "Love your enemies," "Turn the other cheek"—when the notification lit up his phone: his church's prayer chain was celebrating news that ICE had conducted a major raid at a local meatpacking plant, calling it an answer to their prayers for "law and order in our community." He read the Sermon on the Mount again, then read the celebratory messages, and for the first time in his life he couldn't make the two fit together no matter how hard he tried.

The disconnect had been building for weeks. Every Sunday brought another sermon about the need for strength, toughness, and decisive action against "those who threaten our way of life." The language was always wrapped in Scripture—Romans 13 on governing authorities, Old Testament passages about protecting borders, warnings about wolves in sheep's clothing. But when Marcus tried to square these calls for crackdowns and force with Jesus' actual words about enemies and neighbors, the gap kept widening. Jesus had said to love enemies, pray for persecutors, and turn the other cheek. The men at his church were saying that mercy was weakness and compassion was naïveté, that real

71

faith meant backing the hardest possible line against immigrants, protesters, and anyone labeled a threat.

Marcus thought about the families who worked at that plant, people he'd seen at the grocery store, whose kids went to school with his grandchildren. He imagined armed agents sweeping through the facility, separating parents from children, loading workers onto buses while their families waited at home unaware. He tried to picture Jesus celebrating that scene, calling it an answer to prayer, and the image wouldn't come. Instead, he kept seeing the Jesus who ate with tax collectors and sinners, who touched lepers no one else would approach, who told a story about a Samaritan—a despised outsider— as the model of what it means to love your neighbor.

This chapter confronts one of Christian nationalism's most visible and politically potent themes: the fusion of "law and order" rhetoric with claims about biblical authority and God's plan for America. Across the country, pastors and politicians invoke Scripture to justify harsh immigration enforcement, militarized policing, punitive criminal justice policies, and aggressive responses to protest and dissent, treating these positions not as prudential policy choices but as direct expressions of faithfulness. It then applies the Jesus Principle to the concrete realities of these politics—immigration raids that terrorize families, policing that disproportionately harms Black and brown neighborhoods, and criminal justice systems that prioritize punishment over restoration—asking what kind of fruit they bear, whether they protect or harm the vulnerable, how they fare under the Golden Rule, and whether they align with the teaching and example of Jesus.

By the end, Marcus—and readers alongside him—will be forced to choose between the politics of fear and the way of the one who said, "Blessed are the merciful, for they will be shown mercy."

### The Politics of Fear: How "Law and Order" Rhetoric Frames Neighbors as Enemies

The language of "law and order" sounds straightforward, and who could be against safe communities and the rule of law? Yet in American political history, this phrase has functioned less as a neutral description of public safety and more as a powerful rhetorical tool that reshapes how citizens view one another. When political and religious leaders invoke "law and order," they are not simply describing crime statistics or proposing evidence-based safety measures.[29] [30] They are constructing a moral narrative that divides the world into the law-abiding and the lawless, the virtuous and the dangerous, the real Americans and the threats.[29] [31]

This narrative operates through what scholars call the politics of fear, mobilizing voters by emphasizing danger, insecurity, and the need for harsh responses to perceived enemies.[29] [31] Research on political rhetoric shows that fear-based appeals do not simply reflect objective crime rates; they actively shape public perception of threat, often increasing support for punitive policies even when crime is declining.[29] [31]

The transformation from neighbor to enemy happens through a three-step process. First, people are divided into moral categories: law-abiding citizens versus lawbreakers, good people versus criminals.[29] [31] Second, those labeled as lawbreakers are depicted not merely as people who have committed illegal acts but as fundamentally bad, irredeemable, or parasitic.[29] [31] Third, their presence is narrated as an existential threat to "our way of life," "our families," or "our nation," moving them from wrongdoers to enemies.[31] [34] This framing is profoundly relational because it redefines neighbors as potential threats, fundamentally undermining social trust and the possibility of reconciliation.

Throughout American history, "law and order" rhetoric has been deployed strategically to criminalize dissent and marginalize vulnerable communities. During the civil rights era, peaceful demonstrators organizing sit-ins and marches were labeled by officials as "outside agitators" and "lawbreakers," despite their commitment to nonviolent civil disobedience.[77] Public officials framed the movement as a threat to social peace, leading many White Christians to view their Black neighbors' quest for equality as a form of anarchy rather than as a legitimate demand for justice.[77] The language of order was used to defend unjust laws and portray those seeking justice as enemies of society.[77]

In the 1990s, the widely cited but later discredited "superpredator" theory warned of a coming wave of remorseless young criminals, often depicted as Black and Latino males.[32] Although crime rates were actually beginning to decline, this fear-driven narrative led to harsher sentencing laws, increased police presence in schools, and a cultural perception of certain neighborhoods' youth as inherently dangerous rather than as children in need of opportunity and care.[29] [32] The predicted superpredator wave never materialized, and the original theorist publicly recanted, but the damage to communities, trust, and millions of lives was immense.[32]

More recently, immigrants and refugees have been cast as criminals and invaders, protesters for racial justice have been labeled as rioters and anarchists, and political opponents have been depicted as enemies within who must be defeated or silenced.[31] [34] When Christian nationalist rhetoric fuses crime, disorder, and theological deviation, it creates a layered category of the "dangerous unbelieving neighbor"— someone who is simultaneously criminal, politically subversive, and spiritually corrupt.[31] [32] [77] This multi-dimensional enmity makes Jesus' command to love enemies appear naive or even dangerous, replacing the call to reconciliation with a mandate for control.

In Minneapolis, Minnesota, this same "law and order" script has played out with devastating clarity. In early 2026, the Trump administration launched Operation Metro Surge, sending at least 2,000 ICE officers and 1,000 Customs and Border Protection agents into the Twin Cities under the banner of restoring order and enforcing immigration law. Within weeks, federal agents had killed two U.S. citizens: Renée Nicole Macklin Good, a 37-year-old American woman shot by an ICE agent on January 7, and Alex Jeffrey Pretti, a 37-year-old intensive care nurse for the Department of Veterans Affairs, shot by CBP agents on January 24. Officials defended the operation as necessary to protect "law-abiding Americans," even as local residents described living in fear of heavily armed federal officers and watched neighbors and coworkers—citizens and immigrants alike—treated as enemy combatants. Protesters who marched against the killings and the wider surge were quickly denounced by national leaders as "domestic terrorists," confirming the pattern: dissent and calls for accountability were framed not as expressions of democratic responsibility but as threats to be contained.

## Immigration Enforcement, Criminal Justice, and the Sermon on the Mount

Immigration enforcement is a prime testing ground for "law and order" theology. When Christian nationalist leaders invoke "law and order" in the name of biblical faithfulness, they often point to specific policies that promise safety through strength: mass deportations of undocumented immigrants, militarized responses to protest, mandatory minimum sentences, and expanded police powers in communities labeled as high-crime. These measures are framed not as prudential choices among many options but as expressions of God's design for justice, with Romans 13's command to obey governing authorities cited as divine endorsement of whatever force the state chooses to deploy.[79] Yet when these policies are examined in light of the Sermon on the Mount and the actual lives they touch, the gap between Christian nationalist rhetoric and the way of Jesus becomes impossible to ignore.

As Minneapolis residents discovered, Immigration enforcement under Christian nationalist frameworks has increasingly relied on tactics designed to instill fear and maximize removal, regardless of family ties or community roots.[79] Large-scale workplace raids separate parents from children in moments, leaving families fractured and communities traumatized.[79] Research on immigration enforcement shows that such operations produce widespread psychological harm not only for those detained but for entire neighborhoods, where fear of interaction with any authority—including schools and hospitals—rises sharply. Children whose parents are deported experience elevated rates of anxiety, depression, and developmental disruption, outcomes that persist long after the initial separation. When enforcement is celebrated as an answer to prayer for "law and order," the question must be asked: what kind of fruit does this bear in the lives of children and families and other residents?

Criminal justice policies championed by Christian nationalist voices have similarly prioritized punishment over restoration, often with devastating consequences for poor communities and communities of color. Mandatory minimum sentencing laws, three-strikes provisions, and the expansion of prosecutorial discretion have contributed to mass incarceration rates that far exceed those of other democracies. The United States holds nearly one-quarter of the world's prisoners despite having less than five percent of its population. Harsh sentencing does little to improve public safety while inflicting long-term harm on individuals, families, and neighborhoods. Children with incarcerated parents face higher risks of poverty, housing instability, and involvement in the justice system themselves, perpetuating cycles of disadvantage across generations.

The Sermon on the Mount points in the opposite direction from these approaches. Jesus commands his followers to love enemies, pray for persecutors, and refuse retaliation, teaching that directly contradicts the politics of fear and force.[78] When he tells his disciples to turn the other cheek and go the extra mile, he is not describing personal piety alone but modeling a posture toward those who threaten or harm that rejects the logic of domination. His refusal to call down fire on his opponents, his rebuke of Peter's sword in the garden, and his forgiveness from the cross all point in the same direction: the way of Jesus is the way of costly, nonviolent love, not the way of the strongman or the crackdown.

Applying the Jesus Principle to "law and order" politics reveals the contradictions clearly. These policies do not bear the fruit of the Spirit in the lives of those most affected; instead, they produce fear, trauma, and broken families.[79] They do not protect the vulnerable; they harm children, impoverish communities, and fall hardest on those already at the margins. They fail the Golden Rule spectacularly: few who celebrate harsh enforcement would accept the same treatment for their own families caught in similar circumstances. And they rest on misleading claims about safety and deterrence that ignore decades of research showing that punitive approaches often make communities less safe, not more.[80]

Marcus could no longer reconcile the celebration of raids and crackdowns with the Jesus who said, "Blessed are the merciful, for they will be shown mercy." The politics of fear demanded enemies; the Sermon on the Mount demanded love.[78]

## The Jesus Principle Test:
## Does Fear-Based Policy Bear the Fruit of Love?

The Jesus Principle offers a straightforward way to evaluate whether any policy—regardless of how it is packaged or which Scripture verses are cited in its defense—actually reflects the way of Jesus. When applied to the "law and order" politics that Christian nationalism champions, the four questions expose a profound disconnect between fear-based enforcement and the fruit of love that Jesus said would mark his followers.[8 9 32]

**Does it bear the fruit of the Spirit?** Galatians 5:22–23 lists love, joy, peace, patience, kindness, goodness, faithfulness, gentleness, and self-control as the visible evidence of the Spirit's work in a person's life.[8 9 32] These qualities are not abstract virtues but concrete realities that shape relationships and communities. When immigration raids sweep through neighborhoods, the fruit borne in those communities is not peace but terror. Research on the psychological impact of enforcement operations shows that children in immigrant families—including those who are U.S. citizens—experience elevated rates of anxiety, depression, and post-traumatic stress symptoms following raids or parental detention. Parents report that their children become afraid to go to school, refuse to leave the house, or wake up with nightmares about agents taking their family away.

Similarly, policies that prioritize punishment over restoration in criminal justice do not produce the fruit of gentleness, patience, or goodness in the lives of those caught in the system or the communities most affected. Mass incarceration has devastated poor neighborhoods and communities of color, removing parents, disrupting families, and creating cycles of disadvantage that span generations. The United States incarcerates people at rates far exceeding other democracies, yet this approach has not made communities safer or more peaceful.

Instead, it has produced broken families, economic hardship, and deepened mistrust between residents and law enforcement. When the fruit in real lives is fear, trauma, and fractured relationships, the claim that these policies reflect the Spirit's work becomes impossible to sustain.[32]

**Does it care for the vulnerable?** Jesus consistently centered those whom society pushed to the margins: the sick, the poor, the foreigner, the child. He told his followers that whatever they did to "the least of these" they did to him. Fear-based enforcement policies do not protect the vulnerable; they target them.[8][9] Undocumented immigrants are among the most vulnerable people in American society, often working dangerous jobs for low wages with no legal recourse when exploited. Children whose parents are deported face immediate trauma and long-term developmental harm. People trapped in cycles of incarceration—disproportionately poor and Black—are denied access to education, employment, and housing long after they have served their sentences. When policies systematically harm those with the least power and fewest resources, they fail the test of caring for the vulnerable.

**Would I want this done to me or my family?** The Golden Rule forces a simple but devastating question: if the roles were reversed, would those celebrating harsh enforcement accept the same treatment for themselves or their loved ones? Marcus found himself unable to answer yes. He could not imagine celebrating if his own daughter were swept up in a workplace raid, if his grandson were separated from his parents and placed in detention, or if his neighbor faced years in prison for a nonviolent offense with no chance of redemption. The Golden Rule exposes how "law and order" politics demand maximum punishment for "them" while assuming mercy and second chances for "us."

**Is it true?** Fear-based rhetoric relies on exaggeration and selective facts about crime rates, immigrant behavior, and the effectiveness of punitive policies. Decades of research show that harsh sentencing has little effect on overall crime rates and that immigrants—including undocumented immigrants—commit crimes at lower rates than native-born citizens, yet Christian nationalist leaders continue to frame immigrants as invaders and protesters as anarchists.

When Marcus ran "law and order" politics through the Jesus Principle, every question returned the same answer: this does not look like Jesus.[11][32] Marcus closed his Bible and sat in the quiet of his kitchen, the celebratory messages about the raid still glowing on his phone's screen. For the first time, he could not make the Sermon on the Mount and the politics of fear fit together, no matter how many times he read Romans 13 or how loudly his pastor insisted that strength and toughness were biblical virtues. The Jesus who commanded his followers to love enemies, pray for persecutors, and turn the other cheek had left no room for the kind of celebration that greeted armed raids, family separations, and the deliberate infliction of terror on vulnerable communities.

When Christian nationalist leaders invoke "law and order" in Jesus' name, they ask Christians to believe that fear-based crackdowns, militarized enforcement, and punitive justice reflect the heart of the one who told his followers to love enemies, bless those who curse them, and refuse retaliation. Yet immigration raids that traumatize children and shatter families do not bear the fruit of peace, kindness, or gentleness. Criminal justice systems that prioritize punishment over restoration and fall hardest on poor communities and communities of color do not protect the vulnerable. Enforcement policies celebrated by those who would never accept the same treatment for their own families fail the Golden Rule spectacularly, and rhetoric that exaggerates threats and frames neighbors as enemies violates the commitment to truth that Jesus modeled and demanded.

The gap between the way of Jesus and the "law and order" politics that Christian nationalism champions is not a matter of policy nuance or principled disagreement among equally faithful Christians. It is a fundamental conflict between two incompatible visions of discipleship: one rooted in the Sermon on the Mount, the other rooted in the pursuit of dominance through state power. Research on immigration enforcement, militarized policing, and mass incarceration consistently shows that fear-based approaches produce trauma, deepen inequality, and fail to make communities safer. The fruit in real lives—broken families, terrorized neighborhoods, cycles of disadvantage spanning generations—exposes the lie that these policies reflect God's design for justice.

Marcus could no longer ignore what the Jesus Principle revealed. The politics of fear demanded enemies; the Sermon on the Mount demanded love. The strongman promised safety through force; Jesus promised blessing through mercy. Christian nationalism celebrated crackdowns and raids as answers to prayer; Jesus wept over Jerusalem and refused the path of domination even when it led to the cross. The choice was becoming painfully clear: Marcus could continue to align his faith with the tribe that promised strength and order, or he could follow the teacher who said, "Blessed are the merciful, for they will be shown mercy." He could not do both.

# CHAPTER 9.

# FAITH WITHOUT COERCION: SOUL FREEDOM, RELIGIOUS PLURALISM, AND THE SEPARATION OF CHURCH AND STATE

Marcus had been a Baptist his entire life, but it wasn't until he stumbled across a 1612 pamphlet excerpt in his pastor's office—written by Baptist founder Thomas Helwys, who died in prison for defending religious liberty—that he realized his own denomination had been founded on a principle he'd spent years voting against. "The King is a mortal man and not God," Helwys had written to England's monarch, "therefore hath no power over the immortal souls of his subjects," and Marcus sat staring at those words, wondering when Baptists had stopped believing that faith must be free or it isn't faith at all.

The pamphlet had been tucked into a display case commemorating the church's centennial, a relic of a heritage Marcus had never thought to question. He'd always assumed that defending religious freedom meant protecting Christians' right to pray in schools or display the Ten Commandments in courthouses, protecting *his* freedom, really, and the freedom of people who believed like him. But Helwys had argued for something far more radical and costly: that every person, regardless of belief, must be free to follow their own conscience before God without interference from civil authorities. Early Baptists had insisted that kings and governors had no God-given authority to compel worship, punish heresy, or decide whose prayers counted and whose didn't. They had been persecuted, fined, imprisoned, and exiled for that conviction, and they had held it not in spite of their faith in Jesus but because of it.

Marcus thought back to the church meetings and political rallies where he'd heard leaders call for a return to America's "Christian foundations" and for laws that would enshrine "biblical values" in public policy. He'd cheered those calls, believing they were about restoring righteousness and protecting the faith from a hostile culture. But now, reading Helwys's words and remembering the price early Baptists paid to keep government out of the soul's business, he felt a knot tightening in his chest. If his ancestors had fought for the freedom of all consciences—even the freedom to be wrong, even the freedom to worship "one God, three Gods, no God, or 20 Gods," as another early Baptist had put it—then what was he supporting when he voted for leaders who promised to use state power to enforce Christian doctrine on everyone?

The question had been growing louder with each chapter of his journey, but this one felt different. This wasn't about policy details or competing interpretations of Scripture. This was about the nature of faith itself. Could belief be genuine if it was coerced by law? Could worship be authentic if it was mandated by government? And if the answer was no—if real faith had to be free or it wasn't faith at all—then what did that mean for every effort to turn America into a "Christian nation" by legal force?

Marcus knew the arguments on the other side. He'd heard pastors and commentators insist that religious freedom was never meant to protect false religions or secularism, only different expressions of Christianity. He'd heard them say that the founders intended a Christian nation and that separating church and state was a modern distortion. He'd heard them warn that without legal support for Christian values, the culture would collapse into chaos and the church would lose its voice. But sitting in that quiet office, staring at the words of a man who had died in prison rather than let a king control his faith, Marcus couldn't shake the feeling that his tradition had once known something his generation had forgotten: that Jesus never asked Caesar to enforce discipleship, and that handing government the power to decide whose prayers and beliefs were acceptable was a betrayal of the gospel itself, not a defense of it.

This chapter forces Marcus to reckon with what his own heritage had always taught and what the Jesus Principle confirmed: that coerced faith produces bad fruit, harms vulnerable minorities, and violates the way of Jesus at its core.

### Soul Freedom and the Baptist Heritage: When Christians Defended Liberty for All

The principle Marcus discovered in that old pamphlet was not a fringe idea or a modern invention. It stood at the heart of Baptist identity from the beginning, forged in the fires of persecution and grounded in a conviction about the nature of faith itself. Early Baptists argued that because genuine belief must be a free response to God's grace, no earthly power—not king, parliament, or magistrate—could rightly compel worship, punish heresy, or decide whose prayers counted as legitimate. It was theology: the insistence that God alone is Lord of the conscience and that coerced religion is no religion at all.[82][83]

Thomas Helwys made this case in his 1612 treatise *A Short Declaration of the Mystery of Iniquity*, the first book published in English to demand religious liberty for all people.[84][85] Writing to King James I, Helwys declared that the monarch had no authority over the immortal souls of his subjects and that every person—Christian, Jew, Muslim, or heretic—must be free to follow their own conscience without interference from the state.[84][85] For this audacity, Helwys was imprisoned in London's Newgate Prison, where he died around 1616, his body likely dumped in an unmarked grave.[84][85] His crime was not treason or violence but the refusal to grant Caesar power over the soul.

Across the Atlantic, Roger Williams carried the same conviction into the wilderness of colonial America. Banished from Massachusetts Bay Colony in 1635 for preaching that civil authorities had no right to enforce religious conformity, Williams fled through winter snow and founded Providence as a refuge for the persecuted.[85] There, he established the first Baptist church in North America in 1638 and secured a colonial charter in 1644 that guaranteed liberty of conscience for all residents, regardless of belief.[81 83 84 85] Williams introduced the metaphor of a "wall of separation between the garden of the church and the wilderness of the world," arguing that state interference corrupted both religion and government.[81 83 84 85] His Rhode Island experiment welcomed Quakers, Jews, and others driven out of colonies where a single church enjoyed legal privilege and state enforcement.[85]

This heritage was not limited to White Baptists. Gowan Pamphlet, an enslaved African American in 1770s Virginia, preached the gospel in secret despite laws forbidding Black religious gatherings. After gaining his freedom in 1793, Pamphlet led Williamsburg's First Baptist Church and joined the Dover Baptist Association, embodying soul freedom even under the brutal constraints of slavery.[85] His ministry demonstrated that the principle transcended race and power, rooted as it was in the conviction that every person stands directly accountable to God.

By the early 19th century, Baptists had become leading advocates for the First Amendment's religion clauses, insisting that religious liberty was an inalienable right, not a favor granted by government.[84] The 1801 letter from the Danbury Baptist Association to President Thomas Jefferson affirmed this view, prompting Jefferson's famous reply invoking a "wall of separation between Church and State."[84] Baptists understood that when government gained power to favor or enforce religion, it inevitably privileged the majority's theology and persecuted dissenters, turning faith into a tool of control rather than a free response to grace.

Edgar Young Mullins, president of Southern Baptist Theological Seminary from 1899 to 1923, formalized this tradition in his 1908 work *The Axioms of Religion*, declaring soul competency "the distinctive historical significance of the Baptists."[82 83 86] For Mullins, the doctrine meant that every individual possesses both the right and the responsibility to interpret Scripture and approach God without coercion from ecclesiastical or civil authorities.[82] [83] [86] This was not individualism run wild but a theological claim about how faith works: it must be free or it is not faith.

Marcus realized that his own tradition had once understood what he was only now beginning to see, that handing government the power to enforce Christian doctrine betrayed the very nature of discipleship and threatened the freedom of every conscience, believer and unbeliever alike.

## The Fruit of State-Enforced Faith:
## Coercion, Shallow Conversion, and Persecution

Marcus had always believed that if America became more Christian— if prayer returned to schools, if the Ten Commandments hung in courtrooms, if laws reflected biblical values—the nation would flourish and the church would thrive. But the evidence pointed in the opposite direction. Across history and around the world, state-enforced faith had produced not genuine devotion but coercion, shallow conversions driven by fear rather than choice, and persecution of those who refused to conform.

Since the fourth century, when the Roman Empire adopted Christianity as its official religion, every state that defined itself as officially Christian faced the same dilemma: how to enforce holiness through political power.[88] The result was predictable. Non-conformists were labeled heretics or aliens, marginalized by law, and often punished by the state.[88] This pattern repeated itself in medieval Europe, colonial America, and in many Western nations that granted legal privilege to a single Christian tradition, alienating dissenters and replacing voluntary faith with compulsory conformity.[88] The Crusader became the ideal over the evangelist, and the gospel of persuasion gave way to the power of the sword.[90]

Research on contemporary Christian nationalism confirms that state sponsorship of faith diminishes rather than strengthens religious adherence. Cross-national studies show that countries where government enforces or privileges a particular religion tend to have lower rates of Christian belief and practice.[87] When faith is coerced rather than chosen, it loses its appeal.[87] People comply outwardly to avoid penalty while their hearts remain untouched, producing exactly the kind of shallow, performative religion Jesus condemned in the Pharisees. As one scholar observed, coercion and state sponsorship of faith diminish faith's appeal and acceptance; it is more effective and more Christ-like to walk alongside neighbors than to wag a finger in their faces.[87]

The fruit of state-enforced faith extends beyond shallow conversion to active persecution. Christian nationalism fosters support for authoritarian measures designed to punish those who deviate from the prescribed order.[56] Studies show that Christian nationalist beliefs strongly predict support for arresting women who seek abortions, not merely as an expression of anti-abortion conviction but as a means of using state power to enforce a particular ethnocultural hierarchy.[56] This punitive impulse extends to harsher criminal sentences, expanded use of the death penalty, and aggressive policing tactics, especially when directed at racial minorities.[56] The link is clear: Christian nationalism provides ideological justification for state control over bodies and consciences, privileging White Christian identity through law enforcement and surveillance.[56]

Contemporary examples illustrate the pattern. After the overturning of Roe v. Wade in 2022, several Republican-led states proposed laws to arrest women for obtaining abortions, with some Christian leaders citing biblical law as the proper foundation for American jurisprudence.[56] In 2023, Texas counties adopted measures to block residents from traveling out of state for abortion care, potentially requiring cell phone monitoring and police interrogation of pregnant women.[56] These policies, ideologically enabled by Christian nationalist convictions, transform the state into an instrument of religious coercion, surveilling private decisions and punishing dissent.[56]

Christian nationalism has also helped fuel violence and intimidation, from the January 6 Capitol attack to racially motivated shootings justified by appeals to defending Christian civilization.[87] When faith becomes fused with political power and national identity, those who do not conform—religious minorities, secular citizens, racial others—are recast as enemies of God and country, making persecution not merely permissible but righteous.[88]

Marcus understood now what his Baptist forebears had known: coerced faith is not faith at all. It produces fear, not love; conformity, not conversion; and persecution, not witness. Jesus did not recruit Caesar to enforce discipleship, because the kingdom of God advances through persuasion, not coercion, through the Spirit's work in free hearts, not the state's power over captive bodies.[89]

## The Jesus Principle Test:
## Would You Want Another Religion Controlling Your Conscience?

Marcus had spent his entire adult life defending religious freedom, or so he thought. He had signed petitions to protect Christian business owners who refused service based on their beliefs, supported legislation to allow prayer in public schools, and donated to legal funds defending pastors' right to preach without government interference. But as he sat with Helwys's words and the weight of his own tradition's history, a new question crystallized in his mind: would he want someone else's religion wielding the same power over his conscience that he had been voting to give his own?

The question was not hypothetical. If Christian nationalists succeeded in establishing legal frameworks that privileged Christian doctrine—defining marriage by one theological interpretation, restricting reproductive choices based on particular readings of when life begins, mandating prayer or religious instruction in public institutions—they would be handing government a tool that could just as easily be turned against them. Marcus imagined a future America where Muslims, Hindus, or secular humanists held legislative majorities and used the same precedents to enforce their convictions on Christian families. Would he accept a school curriculum that taught his grandchildren that Jesus was merely a prophet, not the Son of God? Would he comply with laws requiring businesses to close on Friday for Muslim prayer or to fund rituals he considered idolatrous? Would he submit to a government that criminalized evangelism as hate speech or banned Christian homeschooling as a threat to social cohesion?

The discomfort Marcus felt imagining these scenarios was precisely the point. The Golden Rule—"Do to others as you would have them do to you"—applied not only to individual relationships but to the structures of power Christians sought to build.[8][32] If he would not want another religion controlling his conscience through law, then he had no right to use law to control the consciences of others, no matter how sincerely he believed his own faith was true.[8][32] This was not relativism or a retreat from truth claims. It was a recognition that genuine faith cannot be produced by coercion and that the state, once empowered to enforce religious doctrine, becomes a threat to everyone's freedom, including the freedom of the majority that grants it that power.[32]

The Jesus Principle exposed the danger clearly. State-enforced faith fails to bear the fruit of the Spirit—producing fear and resentment instead of love and joy—and it harms the vulnerable minorities and dissenters who lack the political power to protect themselves.[9] It violates the Golden Rule by demanding from others a submission to religious authority that the majority would never accept for itself.[8][32] And it contradicts the truth of how faith actually works: as a free gift received by free people, not a legal obligation imposed by force.[32]

Marcus understood now that his tradition's defense of soul freedom was not a compromise with secularism, but a theological conviction rooted in the nature of the gospel itself.[32] Jesus never asked Caesar to enforce discipleship. He never sought state power to compel worship or punish heresy. He built his kingdom through persuasion, sacrifice, and the Spirit's work in human hearts and never through the coercive tools of government. To hand those tools to any religious faction, even his own, was to betray the very freedom that made authentic faith possible. Marcus closed the pamphlet and set it back in the display case, his hands unsteady. For the first time in his life, he understood that the religious freedom he had spent years defending was not the freedom his Baptist ancestors had died for. They had fought for the right of every conscience to stand before God without interference from kings or magistrates, even when that meant protecting the freedom of those they believed were wrong. He had fought for the right of Christians like himself to control public institutions, enforce their theology through law, and treat dissenters as threats to be managed rather than neighbors to be loved. The two visions could not have been more different, and Marcus could no longer pretend they were the same.

Marcus thought about the policies he had supported: laws that would enshrine his theology in public schools, restrict the rights of non-Christians, and punish those who refused to conform to his tradition's moral code. He had believed these measures would protect the faith and restore righteousness to a wayward nation. But now he saw them for what they were: attempts to use government power to accomplish what the Spirit alone could do, trading the costly work of persuasion and witness for the shortcut of legal coercion. Jesus never sought Caesar's help to enforce discipleship. He built his kingdom through sacrifice, service, and the Spirit's work in free hearts, rejecting every offer of political power and every temptation to compel belief through force.

The question Helwys had posed to King James now confronted Marcus with equal force: would he grant government authority over the immortal souls of his neighbors, knowing that the same authority could one day be turned against his own children and grandchildren? Would he demand from others a submission to his faith that he would never accept if another religion held the reins of power? The Golden Rule left no room for evasion. If he would not want Muslims, Hindus, or secular humanists controlling his conscience through law, then he had no right to use law to control theirs, no matter how sincerely he believed his own faith was true.

Marcus stood and walked toward the door, the weight of his tradition's forgotten wisdom pressing on his shoulders. Soul freedom was not a compromise with secularism or a retreat from truth. It was a theological conviction rooted in the gospel's nature itself: that authentic faith can only be real when it is free. His ancestors had known this. Jesus had embodied it. And if Marcus was going to follow Jesus rather than a political tribe, he would have to recover what his generation had lost—the courage to protect every conscience, even those he believed were wrong, because coercion could never produce the kingdom of God.

# CHAPTER 10.

# CHOOSING JESUS OVER TRIBE: A CALL TO PUBLIC DISCIPLESHIP THAT LOOKS LIKE LOVE

Marcus sat alone in his truck in the church parking lot, engine off, watching families stream toward the Sunday service he wasn't sure he could walk into anymore. Nine months ago he'd never questioned whether his church and his faith were the same thing, but now—after all the sermons and prayer chains and Bible studies that had celebrated policies he could no longer square with Jesus—he knew he was standing at a fork in the road, and whichever path he chose would cost him something.

The notebook on the passenger seat told the story of his journey. Page after page of questions, Scripture references, and the four simple tests he'd learned to apply to every political claim wrapped in Jesus' name. Does it bear good fruit? Does it protect the vulnerable? Would I want this for my own family? Is it actually true? Over and over, the Christian nationalist vision he'd been taught to call "biblical" had failed those tests, and not because Marcus had become liberal or lost his faith, but because he'd started measuring political rhetoric against the actual teaching and example of Jesus.

He'd watched abortion bans celebrated as victories for life while maternal mortality climbed and women were turned away from emergency rooms during miscarriages. He'd heard "law and order" preached from the pulpit while immigration raids tore families apart and militarized police responses fell hardest on Black and brown neighborhoods. He'd seen "family values" used to justify policies that drove LGBTQ+ youth toward despair, and "religious liberty" deployed to demand legal privilege for one theological faction while dismissing the conscience rights of everyone else. In every case, the fruit was fear, exclusion, and harm to the people Jesus consistently centered, and in every case, the Golden Rule collapsed the moment Marcus imagined his own daughter, his own grandson, or his own community on the receiving end.

The pattern was unmistakable. Christian nationalism had failed the Jesus test not once or twice but systematically, across every arena where it sought to fuse faith with political power and cultural dominance. It bore the fruit of division rather than the Spirit. It sacrificed the vulnerable to protect the comfortable. It demanded from others what its advocates would never accept for themselves. And it rested on half-truths, selective history, and a version of "biblical values" that required ignoring much of what Jesus actually said and did.

Marcus knew what was at stake. Choosing Jesus over tribe meant he would lose friends, face suspicion in his church, and risk being labeled disloyal by people whose approval had once defined his identity. But the alternative—continuing to call Christian nationalism "faithfulness" when it looked nothing like the Sermon on the Mount—had become impossible. He'd spent too many nights reading the Gospels, too many mornings watching the real-world consequences of policies he'd once cheered, too many conversations imagining his own loved ones caught in the systems he'd been taught to defend.

This final chapter is not an ending but an invitation. Marcus's choice is the choice facing millions of Christians who sense the disconnect between the political religion they've inherited and the Jesus they meet in Scripture. It is a choice between a gospel of dominance and a gospel of love, between pursuing power and the practice of mercy, between tribal loyalty and the way of the cross. The Jesus Principle is not merely a diagnostic tool for evaluating Christian nationalism; it is a compass for the daily work of public discipleship, a framework that can guide every conversation, every vote, every decision about what it means to follow Jesus in a fractured and fearful time.

The question is no longer whether Christian nationalism reflects the way of Jesus. The evidence is clear that it does not. The question now is what comes next, and whether ordinary Christians will choose the teacher over the tribe.

## The Recap:
## How Christian Nationalism Failed the Jesus Test in Every Arena

The notebook on Marcus's passenger seat held nine months of evidence, and flipping through it now felt like reading a case file against an ideology he'd once confused with faithfulness itself. Each arena where Christian nationalism had promised to honor God and restore the nation told the same story: when measured against Jesus' actual teaching and example, the project failed every test.

**Women's bodies had become battlegrounds for control rather than sites of compassion.** Abortion bans celebrated as victories for life produced maternal mortality spikes, emergency room denials during miscarriages, and criminal threats against doctors providing standard care. The policies fell hardest on poor women and women of color, the very populations Jesus consistently centered. Contraception access was restricted even as maternal health infrastructure crumbled. Leaders rejected prevention strategies—like comprehensive sex education and no-cost effective contraception— that are strongly associated with lower rates of unintended pregnancies and abortion, choosing criminal penalties and control over women's bodies instead. When Marcus applied the Golden Rule and imagined his own daughter facing these laws during a pregnancy crisis, the "pro-life" label collapsed under the weight of real harm to real women. The fruit was fear, not flourishing, and the vulnerable were sacrificed to ideology.

**Race and belonging revealed who Christian nationalism considered fully human.** The "real American" rhetoric that sounded neutral in sermons translated into voter suppression targeting Black communities, immigration enforcement that separated families and spread terror, and policing practices that treated brown neighborhoods as occupied territory. The chosenness theology that framed White Christians as rightful owners of the nation demanded that others accept second-class status or leave, even as Jesus' ministry crossed every ethnic and ritual boundary to welcome outsiders.[12] The fruit was division and dispossession, not the beloved community.

**LGBTQ+ youth became collateral damage in culture-war campaigns framed as family protection.** Policies marketed as parental rights stripped support systems from the most vulnerable adolescents, driving rates of depression, anxiety, and suicide attempts sharply upward among queer young people. Research showed that family acceptance cut suicide risk by more than half, yet Christian nationalist rhetoric encouraged rejection in the name of biblical values. When Marcus imagined his own grandson needing one of the library books being banned or facing expulsion from a church youth group for coming out, the Golden Rule exposed how these "protections" targeted children rather than shielded them. The fruit was shame and isolation, not the safety Jesus modeled when he fiercely defended children and welcomed outcasts.

**Law and order politics abandoned the Sermon on the Mount for strongman fantasies.** Immigration raids celebrated in prayer chains, militarized police responses to protest, and punitive criminal justice systems that warehoused the poor all claimed biblical warrant. Yet Jesus had commanded love of enemies, turning the other cheek, and rejecting retaliation. The policies bore the fruit of fear and force, harmed the vulnerable populations Jesus consistently defended, and collapsed under the Golden Rule the moment Marcus imagined his own family caught in an enforcement sweep or facing an unforgiving sentencing regime. The gap between "blessed are the peacemakers" and the politics of domination could not be bridged.

**Religious liberty became a demand for Christian privilege rather than freedom of conscience for all.** Christian nationalism sought to fuse church and state, empower government to enforce theological doctrine, and grant legal advantages to preferred beliefs while marginalizing others.[13] [14] [15] This violated the historic Christian conviction of soul freedom—that authentic faith cannot be coerced—and produced the bad fruit of shallow conversions, persecution of dissenters, and erosion of both church and democracy. Jesus had refused political power and never asked Caesar to enforce discipleship, yet Christian nationalism made seizing state authority central to its mission.

Across all of these arenas, the pattern held. Christian nationalism failed to bear the fruit of the Spirit in public life. It harmed rather than protected the vulnerable. It demanded from others what its advocates would never accept for themselves. And it rested on half-truths, selective history, and a version of biblical values that required ignoring much of what Jesus actually said and did. The ideology had failed the Jesus test not occasionally but systematically, and Marcus could no longer pretend otherwise.

### The Choice: Tribe or Teacher, Power or Love

Marcus had spent his entire adult life believing that faithfulness meant loyalty to his church, to his political tribe, to the vision of a Christian America he'd been taught was synonymous with following Jesus. But the notebook in his lap told a different story. Every page documented a collision between the tribal demands of Christian nationalism and the actual teaching of the rabbi from Nazareth who had commanded his followers to love enemies, welcome strangers, and measure every tree by its fruit.

The choice before him was not between faith and politics, nor between loving Jesus and loving his country. It was between two fundamentally incompatible visions of what it means to be Christian in public. One vision—Christian nationalism—promised power, belonging, and the restoration of a mythical golden age when "real Americans" held uncontested authority. The other—public discipleship rooted in the Jesus Principle—offered no such guarantees of dominance, only the difficult work of bearing witness to a kingdom not built on coercion, tribal purity, or the capture of state power.

Christian nationalism's core appeal is tribal. It defines the nation by ethnic and religious homogeneity, elevating shared ancestry, culture, and theological uniformity as the foundation of political community.[8] [9 10] Scholars have documented how this framework prioritizes national self-interest and separation to preserve order, often echoing segregationist logic that treats ethnic boundaries as divinely ordained and immutable.[9 10] This is power through coercion: the state becomes the instrument for imposing one faction's vision of biblical law on everyone else, backed by legal penalty or even violence.

Jesus' teaching moves in the opposite direction. The parable of the Good Samaritan subverts ethnic prejudice by making a despised outsider the hero and redefining "neighbor" to include anyone in need, regardless of tribe. The Sermon on the Mount commands love of enemies and turning the other cheek, explicitly rejecting retaliation and the pursuit of dominance. When offered political power in the wilderness temptations, Jesus refused; when his followers tried to make him king by force, he withdrew. His kingdom, he told Pilate, is not of this world, it does not advance through the mechanisms of earthly rule.[10 91] The early church grew not by seizing the levers of Roman government but through costly, Spirit-led witness that persuaded rather than compelled.[10 32]

The historical fruit of fusing tribe and power under Christian labels has been hollow faith, hypocrisy, and violence. Baptist theologians have long warned that state-enforced religion produces "arrangements where everything is Christian except the actual people," baptizing the status quo and deadening genuine faith.[32] Contemporary critics describe Christian nationalist visions as "fascism cloaked in Christian terminology," noting how calls for revolt to impose a Christian commonwealth over entire populations betray Jesus' model of sacrificial love.[31]

Marcus understood that choosing Jesus over tribe would cost him. Friends would question his loyalty. Church leaders might label him compromised or liberal. The tribal belonging that had once felt like faithfulness would be withdrawn. But the alternative—continuing to call Christian nationalism "biblical" when it systematically failed every test Jesus gave for recognizing true discipleship—had become impossible.

The Jesus Principle offered a different path: measure every political claim by its fruit, its treatment of the vulnerable, its consistency with the Golden Rule, and its alignment with truth. This was not a retreat from public life but a reorientation toward public discipleship that looked like the teacher rather than the tribe, that chose love over the pursuit of power, and that trusted the Spirit's work of transformation over the state's capacity for coercion. Marcus closed the notebook and opened the truck door, ready to walk a narrower road.

## What Comes Next: Practical Steps for Public Discipleship That Looks Like Jesus

Marcus knew the questions before him were no longer theoretical. The Jesus Principle had exposed the gap between Christian nationalism and the way of Jesus—a moral shadow—but diagnosis alone was not discipleship. What mattered now was the daily, concrete work of following Jesus in public life, in conversations, in community, and in the choices that shape both church and society. This work would require practical steps that any believer could take, regardless of position or influence, to embody a public faith that resembled Jesus more than the surrounding culture.

**Start with the four questions as a daily filter.** The Jesus Principle is not a one-time audit but a repeatable framework for every political claim, every sermon illustration, every social media post that invokes Jesus' name. It simply asks whether any belief or action is moving you closer to the character and teachings of Jesus or further away. Before sharing, endorsing, or voting, Marcus learned to pause and ask:

- Does this bear the fruit of the Spirit in the lives it touches?
- Does it protect or harm vulnerable neighbors?
- Would I want this policy applied to my own family?
- Is it actually true, or does it rest on selective facts and half-told history?

These questions, applied consistently, cut through partisan noise and tribal loyalty to reveal whether a proposal reflects Jesus' teaching or merely borrows his name. If you'd like a step-by-step introduction to how the Jesus Principle works and how to practice it, see my earlier book, *The Jesus Principle: Are You Moving Toward Jesus—or Away?*

**Seek out relationships across political and racial lines.** Christian nationalism thrives on homogeneity and the fear of "the other," but Jesus' ministry crossed every boundary his culture considered sacred.[9] [10] Public discipleship requires intentional friendships with people whose experiences and perspectives differ from one's own, across race, class, immigration status, and political affiliation. These relationships are not projects or evangelistic targets but genuine encounters that humanize those whom nationalist rhetoric casts as threats.

**Reframe conversations in your own congregation.** Small groups, Sunday school classes, and church committees are often where Christian nationalist talking points are repeated uncritically. Marcus began gently introducing the Jesus Principle into these spaces, not as a weapon to shame others but as an invitation to measure every claim by Jesus' actual teaching. When someone repeated a slogan about "taking America back," he asked, "What would that look like if we ran it through the fruit of the Spirit test?" When immigration enforcement was celebrated, he wondered aloud, "How does this care for the vulnerable, and would we want it applied to our own families?" These questions do not require expertise or confrontation; they simply redirect attention from tribal loyalty to the way of Jesus, creating space for others to notice the same tensions Marcus had discovered.

**Resist harmful policies while loving neighbors.** Public discipleship is not passive. It includes advocacy, voting, and public witness that protect the vulnerable and resist policies that fail the Jesus test. This might mean contacting elected officials about maternal health funding, supporting organizations that serve immigrant families, or speaking up when church leaders endorse candidates or platforms that systematically harm marginalized communities. Resistance rooted in the Jesus Principle does not demonize opponents but insists that love, justice, and truth matter more than partisan victory. Historical examples—from abolitionists to civil rights activists—demonstrate that Christians have long practiced public discipleship by challenging unjust systems while refusing to abandon the posture of enemy-love that Jesus commanded.

**Choose the Great Commission over cultural conquest.** Christian nationalism trades the call to make disciples for a project of legal control and cultural dominance.[8][9][10][11] In practice it has already weakened Christian witness: denominations most closely identified with Christian nationalist politics, like the Southern Baptist Convention, have lost millions of members in recent years even as their leaders have doubled down on partisan alignment and "biblical values" campaigns. Public discipleship returns to Jesus' actual mission: bearing witness to the kingdom through transformed lives, not coerced conformity.[32] This means prioritizing evangelism, mercy, and Spirit-led persuasion over the pursuit of state power, trusting that authentic faith spreads through love rather than legislation.

Marcus realized that recovering the gospel required disentangling it from nationalist projects, so that the watching world could see Jesus clearly again, not as a tribal mascot but as the Lord who calls all people to follow him freely.

Marcus finally stepped out of the truck and walked toward the church doors, but this time he carried something new: the clarity that following Jesus and defending Christian nationalism were not the same thing, and the courage to choose the teacher over the tribe. The journey documented in his notebook had not made him less Christian or less committed to living his faith in public; it had simply forced him to ask whether the political religion he had inherited actually resembled the rabbi from Nazareth who commanded enemy-love, centered the marginalized, and refused the path of coercion and dominance.

The case against Christian nationalism is ultimately a case *for* Jesus. Across every arena examined in this book—women's bodies, race and belonging, LGBTQ+ youth, law and order, and church-state fusion—the ideology failed the four-question test not because it was evaluated by secular standards or progressive politics, but because it was measured against the actual teaching and example of the one whose name it claims.

In the end, the invitation is the same one Marcus faced in the parking lot: to disentangle faith from political tribe and commit to a public discipleship that looks like Jesus in both substance and tone. It means seeking out relationships across political and racial lines, humanizing those whom nationalist rhetoric casts as threats, and practicing the Golden Rule in concrete encounters rather than abstract theory. It means reframing conversations in congregations and small groups, gently redirecting attention from tribal loyalty to the way of Jesus, and creating space for others to notice the tensions between Christian nationalism and Christian discipleship.

Public discipleship also requires resistance. Love of neighbor includes advocacy, voting, and public witness that protect the vulnerable and challenge policies that fail the Jesus test. This resistance does not demonize opponents or retreat into private piety; it insists that justice, mercy, and truth matter more than partisan victory, and it trusts that the kingdom advances through Spirit-led transformation rather than state-enforced conformity. The Great Commission calls Christians to make disciples, not to capture legislatures, and the watching world will recognize Jesus' followers not by their political dominance but by their love in action.

The fork in the road is real, and the cost of choosing Jesus over tribe is not trivial. Friends will question loyalty. Church leaders may withdraw approval. The belonging that once felt like isolation or conflict may replace faithfulness. But the alternative—continuing to call Christian nationalism "biblical" when it systematically betrays the teaching of Jesus—has become untenable for anyone who takes the Gospels seriously. The Jesus Principle is not merely a diagnostic tool for evaluating an ideology; it is a compass for the lifelong work of following Jesus in public, a framework that can guide every conversation, every vote, every decision about what it means to bear witness to a kingdom not built on coercion, tribal purity, or the pursuit of power. Marcus closed his notebook and walked toward the church, ready to choose love over dominance, truth over slogans, and Jesus over every competing claim to his allegiance.

-----

For a fuller guide to living with that compass in daily life—in church, at home, and in the voting booth—*The Jesus Principle: Are You Moving Toward Jesus—or Away?* is meant to be a companion volume to this one and is available on Amazon.

# BIBLIOGRAPHY

## References

[1] Butler, K. (2024, October). *Inside the New Apostolic Reformation: The Christian Nationalist Movement That Aspires to Take Over Government.* Mother Jones. https://www.motherjones.com/politics/2024/10/new-apostolic-reformation-christian-nationalism/

[2] Pew Research Center. (2024, March 15). *Christianity's place in politics, and 'Christian nationalism'.* Pew Research Center. https://www.pewresearch.org/religion/2024/03/15/christianitys-place-in-politics-and-christian-nationalism/

[3] Kaylor, B., & Underwood, B. (2024, June 25). *Civil religion as a gateway to Christian nationalism.* Religion News Service. https://religionnews.com/2024/06/25/civil-religion-as-a-gateway-to-christian-nationalism/

[4] Klink, M. (2020, October 19). *Taking America Back for God: Christian Nationalism in the United States | Andrew L. Whitehead & Samuel L. Perry.* Pastor Theologians. https://www.pastortheologians.com/book-reviews-archive/2020/10/19/taking-america-back-for-god

[5] Volf, M. (2020, July 1). *Taking America Back for God.* Yale Center for Faith & Culture. https://faith.yale.edu/media/taking-america-back-for-god

[6] Keller, T. (n.d.). *A Book Review on the Topic of Christian Nationalism.* Gospel in Life. https://gospelinlife.com/article/book-review-on-the-topic-of-christian-nationalism/

[7] SundaytoSaturday.com. (2022, November 21). *SERMON: Taking America Back for God?.* Sunday to Saturday. https://sundaytosaturday.com/2022/11/21/sermon-taking-america-back-for-god/

[8] Shenvi, N. (n.d.). *Of Gods and Men: A Long Review of Wolfe's Case for Christian Nationalism, Part I: Book Summary.* Neil Shenvi - Apologetics.

https://shenviapologetics.com/of-gods-and-men-a-long-review-of-wolfes-case-for-christian-nationalism-part-i-book-summary/

[9] Reason.com. (2023, May 13). *Beware the Christian Prince*. Reason.com. https://reason.com/2023/05/13/beware-the-christian-prince/

[10] Littlejohn, B. (n.d.). *The Case for Christian Nationalism*. The Gospel Coalition. https://www.thegospelcoalition.org/themelios/review/the-case-for-christian-nationalism/

[11] Luke, S. (2024, February 23). *The Case Against Christian Nationalism: Response to Stephen Wolfe (Part 1)*. Pursuing God's Thoughts. https://thinkinghisthoughts.wordpress.com/2024/02/23/the-case-against-christian-nationalism-response-to-stephen-wolfe-part-1/

[12] Whitehead, A. L. (2025, September 11). *Five Elements of Christian Nationalism*. Kettering Foundation. https://kettering.org/five-elements-of-christian-nationalism/

[13] Volle, A. (2025, November 10). *Christian nationalism*. Britannica. https://www.britannica.com/topic/Christian-nationalism

[14] Leadingham, S. A. (2024, March 4). *What Is Christian Nationalism? The Complete Guide*. Freedom Forum. https://www.freedomforum.org/what-is-christian-nationalism/

[15] Pew Research Center. (2022, October 27). *Views of the U.S. as a 'Christian nation' and opinions about 'Christian nationalism'*. Pew Research Center. https://www.pewresearch.org/religion/2022/10/27/views-of-the-u-s-as-a-christian-nation-and-opinions-about-christian-nationalism/

[16] Schreiner, P. (n.d.). *The Good, the Bad, and the Ugly of Christian Nationalism*. The Gospel Coalition. https://www.thegospelcoalition.org/article/good-bad-ugly-christian-nationalism/

[17] Christians Against Christian Nationalism. (n.d.). *What is Christian nationalism?*. Christians Against Christian Nationalism. https://www.christiansagainstchristiannationalism.org/learn-more

[18] Oxford University Press. (n.d.). *Article Navigation.* Sociology of Religion. https://academic.oup.com/socrel/advance-article/doi/10.1093/socrel/srae029/7841527?searchresult=1

[19] Frazer, G. (n.d.). *The Faith of the Founding Fathers.* The Master's University. https://www.masters.edu/mastertmunews/the-faith-of-the-founding-fathers/

[20] Till, F. (n.d.). *The Christian Nation Myth.* Internet Infidels. https://infidels.org/library/modern/the-christian-nation-myth/

[21] Flick, S. (2025, July 2). *Christian Quotes from the Founding Fathers.* Christian Heritage Fellowship. https://christianheritagefellowship.com/christian-quotes-from-the-founding-fathers-2/

[22] Mohn, E. (2022). *Christian nationalism.* EBSCO Research Starters. https://www.ebsco.com/research-starters/religion-and-philosophy/christian-nationalism

[23] The General Board of Church and Society. (n.d.). *Christian Nationalism in the U.S..* The General Board of Church and Society. https://www.umcjustice.org/latest/christian-nationalism-in-the-u-s-1933

[24] Johnston, T. (2018, November 27). *Four Types of Questions in Christ's Dialogical Method.* The Trivium Institute. https://www.triviuminstitute.net/single-post/2018/11/27/four-types-of-questions-in-christs-dialogical-method

[25] Rohrer, S. (2025, November 13). *4 Questions Which Lead to Truth.* Stand in the Gap Media. https://standinthegapmedia.org/2025/11/4-questions-which-lead-to-truth/

[26] Contra Mundum. (2025, December 11). *Contra Mundum.* Captivate.fm. https://feeds.captivate.fm/contramundum/

[27] Harris, J. (n.d.). *Conversations That Matter.* RedCircle. https://redcircle.com/conversations-that-matter8971

[28] Bernardo, A. (2025, December 16). *Ep 234: Biblical Masculinity and the Men of Genesis with Eric Schansberg*. The Protestant Libertarian Podcast. https://feeds.buzzsprout.com/1978104.rss

[29] Bird, M. F. (2024, April 8). *Review of Stephen Wolfe's The Case for Christian Nationalism*. Word from the Bird. https://michaelfbird.substack.com/p/review-of-stephen-wolfes-the-case

[30] Wilsey, J. D. (2023, April 28). *The Christian Prince Against the Dad Bod: An Assessment of The Case for Christian Nationalism*. The London Lyceum. https://thelondonlyceum.com/book-review-the-case-for-christian-nationalism-stephen-wolfe/

[31] 9siduri. (2024, August 5). *Review of "The Case Against Christian Nationalism: An Expository Commentary on Stephen Wolfe's Book" by Blake Callens*. Reviews of Old and New Stories. Mostly Old. https://dmlongrie.com/2024/08/05/review-of-the-case-against-christian-nationalism-an-expository-commentary-on-stephen-wolfes-book-by-blake-callens/

[32] Walker, A. T. (2022, December 9). *Book Review: The Case for Christian Nationalism, by Stephen Wolfe*. 9Marks. https://www.9marks.org/article/a-baptist-engagement-with-the-case-for-christian-nationalism/

[33] Potter, C. (2025, September 8). *A Case for Christian Nationalism: Review*. Creational Story. https://creationalstory.com/a-case-for-christian-nationalism-review/

[34] DeYoung, K. (n.d.). *The Rise of Right-Wing Wokeism: A Review of Stephen Wolfe's The Case for Christian Nationalism*. The Gospel Coalition. https://www.thegospelcoalition.org/reviews/christian-nationalism-wolfe/

[35] Lausanne Movement. (n.d.). *Christian Denominations*. Lausanne Movement. https://lausanne.org/report/polycentric-christianity/christian-denominations

[36] Wikipedia. (n.d.). *Christianity by country*. Wikipedia. https://en.wikipedia.org/wiki/Christianitybycountry

[37] Wikipedia. (n.d.). *List of Christian denominations by number of members.* Wikipedia. https://en.wikipedia.org/wiki/ListofChristiandenominationsbynumberof_members

[38] Ervin, M. (n.d.). *Number of Christian Denominations.* The Third Well. https://www.thirdwell.org/Number-of-Christian-Denominations.html

[39] D. A. Carson, "Interpreting Women's Roles: A Study of 1 Timothy 2 in the Modern Context," The Gospel Coalition, April 9, 2024, accessed January 27, 2026, https://www.thegospelcoalition.org/sermon/church-teaching-authority-in-context-of-1-timothy-2/[40] Paulson, S. (2024, May 3). *A Christian Nationalist Versus a Woman Voter: Reading the Bible Differently.* Westar Institute. https://www.westarinstitute.org/blog/a-christian-nationalist-versus-a-woman-voter-reading-the-bible-differently

[40] Timothy 2:12; see also John Piper and Wayne Grudem, eds., *Recovering Biblical Manhood and Womanhood: A Response to Evangelical Feminism* (Wheaton, IL: Crossway, 1991), 35–52.

[41] Beamish, K. (n.d.). *Why Christian Nationalism Is a Feminist Issue.* National Organization for Women. https://now.org/blog/why-christian-nationalism-is-a-feminist-issue/

[42] Deckman, M. (2023, March 27). *Not Just Proud Boys: Women Espouse Christian Nationalist Views Too.* PRRI. https://prri.org/spotlight/not-just-proud-boys-women-espouse-christian-nationalist-views-too/

[43] Allen D. Hertzke, "Religious Agency and the Integration of Marginalized People," in Christianity and Freedom, Volume 2: Contemporary Perspectives, ed. Allen D. Hertzke (Cambridge: Cambridge University Press, 2016), 272–76.

[44] Oxford University Press. (n.d.). *Article Navigation.* Sociology of Religion. https://academic.oup.com/socrel/advance-article/doi/10.1093/socrel/srae045/8064620?searchresult=1

[45] Graves-Fitzsimmons, G. (n.d.). *Christian Nationalism Is 'Single Biggest Threat' to America's Religious Freedom.* Center for American Progress.

https://www.americanprogress.org/article/christian-nationalism-is-single-biggest-threat-to-americas-religious-freedom/

[46] CUNY SPH. (2025, July 1). *Forecasting how abortion bans affect maternal mortality and morbidity.* CUNY School of Public Health. https://sph.cuny.edu/life-at-sph/news/2025/07/01/abortion-bans-maternal-mortality/

[47] Gender Equity Policy Institute. (2025, April). *Maternal Mortality in the United States After Abortion Bans: Mothers Living in Abortion Ban States at Significantly Higher Risk of Death During Pregnancy and Childbirth.* The GEPI. https://thegepi.org/maternal-mortality-abortion-bans/

[48] PRB. (n.d.). *Abortion Bans Linked to Sharp Rise in Sepsis, Infant Death, and Pregnancy-Associated Deaths, New Research Shows.* Population Reference Bureau. https://www.prb.org/articles/abortion-bans-linked-to-sharp-rise-in-sepsis-infant-death-and-maternal-mortality-new-research-shows/

[49] Lantz, P. M. (2025, October 24). *The Impact of Restrictive State Abortion Laws: State of the Research Evidence in 2025.* Milbank Quarterly. https://www.milbank.org/quarterly/opinions/the-impact-of-restrictive-state-abortion-laws-state-of-the-research-evidence-in-2025/

[50] Johns Hopkins Bloomberg School of Public Health. (2025, February 13). *Two New Studies Provide Broadest Evidence to Date of Unequal Impacts of Abortion Bans.* Johns Hopkins Bloomberg School of Public Health. https://publichealth.jhu.edu/2025/two-new-studies-provide-broadest-evidence-to-date-of-unequal-impacts-of-abortion-bans

[51] Zori, G., Case, S., Pyche, C., & Beckman, L. (2025, August 14). *The relationship between state-level abortion policy and maternal mortality in the United States: a scoping review.* PubMed Central. https://pmc.ncbi.nlm.nih.gov/articles/PMC12352390/

[52] Gender Equity Policy Institute. "Maternal Mortality in the United States After Abortion Bans: Mothers Living in Abortion Ban States at Significantly Higher Risk of Death During Pregnancy and Childbirth." Los Angeles: Gender Equity Policy Institute, April 2025.

[53] The Independent. (n.d.). *Trump, Christian nationalism and the fight over abortion access in America.* The Independent. https://www.the-independent.com/news/world/americas/us-politics/trump-christian-nationalism-abortion-ban-b2629614.html

[54] Lee, C. N. (2024, February 28). *A Thousand Little Moments: The Insidious Loss of Women's Freedom to Christian Nationalism.* Ms. Magazine. https://msmagazine.com/2024/02/28/women-choice-freedom-republicans-religion-ivf-fertility/

[55] O'Connor, K. (2025, November 5). *Pronatalism: Just White Christian Nationalism in Disguise.* National Women's Law Center. https://nwlc.org/pronatalism-just-white-christian-nationalism-in-disguise/

[56] Oxford University Press. (n.d.). *Article Navigation.* Social Problems. https://academic.oup.com/socpro/advance-article/doi/10.1093/socpro/spaf030/8178223

[57] Stone, R. M. (2015, November). *The Politics of Contraception.* Sojourners. https://sojo.net/magazine/november-2015-0/politics-contraception

[58] Oxford University Press. (n.d.). *Chapter Abstract.* Oxford Academic. https://academic.oup.com/book/41502/chapter/352915832

[59] Yale University. (2022, October 4). *Understanding White Christian Nationalism.* Institution for Social and Policy Studies at Yale. https://isps.yale.edu/news/blog/2022/10/understanding-white-christian-nationalism

[60] White, R. (2017, March 22). *Christian Nation.* Boston Review. https://www.bostonreview.net/articles/richard-white-christian-nation/

[61] Harvard Divinity School. (2020, August 20). *How White Evangelicals Tour the Nation's Capital and Redeem a Christian America.* Harvard Divinity School. https://www.hds.harvard.edu/news/2020/08/20/how-white-evangelicals-tour-nations-capital-and-redeem-christian-america

[62] Wikipedia. (n.d.). *Christian nationalism in the United States*. Wikipedia. https://en.wikipedia.org/wiki/ChristiannationalismintheUnited_Stat es

[63] The Cairo Review of Global Affairs. (2023, February 8). *Fear and Power: Christian Nationalism in America*. The Cairo Review of Global Affairs. https://www.thecairoreview.com/essays/fear-and-power-christian-nationalism-in-america/

[64] Woodrum, J. (2023, November 13). *The danger of Christian nationalism*. ACLU of South Carolina. https://www.aclusc.org/news/danger-christian-nationalism/

[65] Richards Augros, G. (2023, May 9). *The Dog Whistle of "Christian Nationalism"*. The Heritage Foundation. https://www.heritage.org/conservatism/commentary/the-dog-whistle-christian-nationalism

[66] Dickerman, P. (2024, December 11). *The New Antebellum: A Sociological Interpretation of Christian Nationalism and its Danger to Both Christianity and American Democracy*. Ursinus College. https://www.ursinus.edu/live/files/5405-paige-dickerman-2025-schellhase-ethics-honorable

[67] Defense of Democracy. (2025, July 22). *Traditional Family Values*. Defense of Democracy. https://defenseofdemocracy.org/dofd-wiki/dog-whistle-dictionary/traditional-family-values/

[68] Lilman, S. (2025, August 12). *Christian Nationalist 'family values' exclude lots of families*. Americans United for Separation of Church and State. https://www.au.org/the-latest/articles/christian-nationalist-family-values-exclude-lots-of-families/

[69] Oxford University Press. (n.d.). *Article Navigation*. Social Forces. https://academic.oup.com/sf/advance-article/doi/10.1093/sf/soaf058/8120584

[70] Wikipedia. (n.d.). *Christian nationalism*. Wikipedia. https://en.wikipedia.org/wiki/Christian_nationalism

[71] Harris, L. (2020, July 16). *'It Breaks the Heart of God' Say Faith Leaders on LGBTQ+ Youth Suicide Rates*. Sojourners.

https://sojo.net/articles/news/it-breaks-heart-god-say-faith-leaders-LGBTQ+-youth-suicide-rates

[72] Williams Institute. (2023, December 20). *LGBTQ+ people raised Christian report more minority stressors, similar health to those who were not.* Williams Institute. https://williamsinstitute.law.ucla.edu/press/LGBTQ+-christianity-press-release/

[73] Upenieks, L., & Hill, T. D. (2023, December 7). *Christian nationalism, religious struggles, and the structural amplification of emotional distress.* Social Science Quarterly. https://onlinelibrary.wiley.com/doi/10.1111/ssqu.13327

[74] James, I. (2023, October 2). *Fighting forward: LGBTQ++ young people are under attack. In addition to nasty politics, blame a resurgence of Christian Nationalism.* Americans United for Separation of Church and State. https://www.au.org/the-latest/church-and-state/articles/fighting-forward-LGBTQ+-young-people-are-under-attack-in-addition-to-nasty-politics-blame-a-resurgence-of-christian-nationalism/

[75] Posner, S. (2022, September 21). *Christian Nationalism and Anti-Trans Laws.* Type Investigations. https://www.typeinvestigations.org/investigation/2022/09/21/christian-nationalism-anti-trans-laws/

[76] Upenieks, L. (2022, February 25). *Do Beliefs in Christian Nationalism Predict Mental Health Problems? The Role of Religious (Non)Involvement.* Socius: Sociological Research for a Dynamic World. https://journals.sagepub.com/doi/10.1177/23780231221081641

[77] Clark, J. (2022, November). *Book Review: "The Case for Christian Nationalism".* The North American Anglican. https://northamanglican.com/book-review-the-case-for-christian-nationalism/

[78] Jenkins, J. (2024, September 30). *Vance, at Christian nationalist revival, says immigration stance is in keeping with faith.* National Catholic Reporter. https://www.ncronline.org/news/vance-christian-nationalist-revival-says-immigration-stance-keeping-faith

[79] AU Staff Member. (2024, October 8). *My journey from immigrant rights to church-state separation*. Americans United for Separation of Church and State. https://www.au.org/the-latest/articles/immigrant-rights-christian-nationalism/

[80] Pinkoski, N. (n.d.). *Immigration for Christians*. Center for Renewing America. https://americarenewing.com/immigration-for-christians/

[81] Hollman, K. H. (2008, April 27). *Foundations of Religious Freedom*. College Park Baptist Church. https://collegeparkchurch.com/foundations-of-religious-freedom/

[82] Evans, F. (2021, December 7). *Free to Be or Free to Believe? What the Battle for Baptist Identity Tells Us About Religious Liberty*. Ad Fontes Journal. https://adfontesjournal.com/web-exclusives/free-to-be-or-free-to-believe-what-the-battle-for-baptist-identity-tells-us-about-religious-liberty/

[83] Gender Equity Policy Institute. "Maternal Mortality in the United States After Abortion Bans: Mothers Living in Abortion Ban States at Significantly Higher Risk of Death During Pregnancy and Childbirth." Los Angeles: Gender Equity Policy Institute, April 2025.

[84] MBC Pathway. (2019, October 14). *Our Baptist heritage: freedom of conscience*. MBC Pathway. https://mbcpathway.com/2019/10/14/our-baptist-heritage-freedom-of-conscience/

[85] BJC. (n.d.). *Baptist Freedom Fighters*. BJC. https://bjconline.org/mission-history-baptist-heritage/

[86] Pinson, W. M., Jr. (2025, February 25). *Is Soul Competency The Baptist Distinctive?*. Center for Baptist History and Heritage. https://www.dbu.edu/baptist-heritage/articles/is-soul-competency-the-baptist-distinctive/index.html

[87] Lagerwey, C. (2025, March 5). *How to End Christian Nationalism*. Reformed Journal. https://reformedjournal.com/2025/03/05/45594/

[88] Whittock, M. (n.d.). *Is 'Christian nationalism' a contradiction in terms?*. Psephizo. https://www.psephizo.com/life-ministry/is-christian-nationalism-a-contradiction-in-terms/

[89] Fitch, D. (2023, November 21). *Why Christian Nationalism is anathema to the mission of God*. Fitch's Provocations. https://davidfitch.substack.com/p/why-christian-nationalism-is-anathema

[90] Rich, A. (2024, December 18). *Christian Nationalism: A Dangerous Heresy*. First Fruits of Zion. https://ffoz.org/messiah/articles/christian-nationalism-a-dangerous-heresy

[91] RamistThomist. (2023, December 13). *The Case for Christian Nationalism, a review*. Puritan Board. https://puritanboard.com/threads/the-case-for-christian-nationalism-a-review.112609/

www.ingramcontent.com/pod-product-compliance
Lightning Source LLC
Chambersburg PA
CBHW022101020426
42335CB00012B/786